WHAT'S WRONG WITH BENEVOLENCE

WHAT'S WRONG WITH BENEVOLENCE

Happiness, Private Property, and the Limits of Enlightenment

David Stove

Edited by Andrew Irvine

Foreword by Roger Kimball

ENCOUNTER BOOKS

NEW YORK · LONDON

First American edition published in 2011 by Encounter Books, an activity of Encounter for Culture and Education, Inc., a nonprofit, tax exempt corporation.
Encounter Books website address: www.encounterbooks.com

Manufactured in the United States and printed on acid-free paper. The paper used in this publication meets the minimum requirements of ANSI/NISO Z39.48 1992 (R 1997) (*Permanence of Paper*).

FIRST AMERICAN EDITION

LIBRARY OF CONGRESS CATALOGING-IN-PUBLICATION DATA

Stove, D. C. (David Charles)
What's wrong with benevolence : happiness, private property, and the limits of enlightenment / by David Stove ; edited by Andrew Irvine ; foreword by Roger Kimball.
p.   cm.
Includes bibliographical references and index.
ISBN-13: 978-1-59403-523-4 (hardcover : alk. paper)
ISBN-10: 1-59403-523-7 (hardcover : alk. paper)
1. Benevolence. 2. Public welfare—Philosophy.
I. Irvine, A. D. II. Title.
BJ1474.S76 2011
177'.7—dc22
2010041447

10 9 8 7 6 5 4 3 2 1

For David and Jenny Armstrong

CONTENTS

FOREWORD

The most melancholy of human reflections, perhaps, is that, on the whole, it is a question whether the benevolence of mankind does most good or harm. Great good, no doubt, philanthropy does, but then it also does great evil. It augments so much vice, it multiplies so much suffering, it brings to life such great populations to suffer and to be vicious, that it is open to argument whether it be or be not an evil to the world, and this is entirely because excellent people fancy they can do much by rapid action – that they will most benefit the world when they most relieve their own feelings.

WALTER BAGEHOT

Benevolence is the heroin of the Enlightened.

DAVID STOVE

THE MOST THRILLING intellectual discovery of my adult life came in 1996 when I chanced upon the work of the Australian philosopher David Stove (1927–1994). I have recounted the details of that discovery, and the reasons for my excitement, in the introduction to *Against the Idols of the Age,** the anthology of Stove's work that I edited in the late 1990s. Here it will suffice to say that I found Stove's combination of philosophical insight, polemical bravura, and

---

* "Who Was David Stove?" in *Against the Idols of the Age*, by David Stove, ed. Roger Kimball (New Brunswick: Transaction Publishers, 1999), pp. vii–xxxii.

astringent impatience with political correctness as novel as it was refreshing. Stove brought an extraordinarily keen intellect, bolstered by commanding historical scholarship, to bear on subjects as diverse as the philosophy of science, philosophical idealism, and neo-Darwinian orthodoxy, not to mention a wide range of topical issues. The spectacle of rigorous cognitive activity – bristling arguments deployed in the service of truth – was gratifying to behold.

There was also the attraction of his prose. David Stove was a stylist of the first water. Reading him, said one admirer, is "like watching Fred Astaire dance." The union of skill and seeming effortlessness is a thing of beauty. Stove could also be extremely funny – assuming, that is, that you were not the object of his scarifying wit: "The Faculty of Arts at the University of Sydney," he wrote in one essay, "is a disaster-area, and not of the merely passive kind, like a bombed building, or an area that has been flooded. It is the active kind, like a badly-leaking nuclear reactor, or an outbreak of foot-and-mouth disease in cattle." Stove went on to quote from, and ridicule, the work of several of his colleagues. He cheerfully identified one egregious offender by name, concluding that, intellectually, "the sum of Marxism, semiotics, and feminism is $0 + 0 + 0 = 0$." True, all true, but hardly balm for the advocates of Marxism, semiotics, feminism, and the rest of what Stove rightly called the intellectual "slums."

The present work, written toward the end of Stove's life, looks behind the smiling, self-satisfied countenance of modern Western societies – all those plump beneficiaries of Enlightened aspiration, instinctively committed to secularism, utilitarianism, and everything compassed by the emetic phrase "social justice." We who enjoy the many perquisites of those societies – the staggering affluence, the cornucopia of indulgence – seldom ask what stands behind it and whether it is (to poach a term from the snippy lexicon of the environmentalists) sustainable.

David Stove rather specialized in embarking on such disobliging inquiries. Imagine writing a book that explodes the intellectual claims of Thomas "Mr. Paradigm Change" Kuhn, that darling of *bien-pensants* cognophobes everywhere! Imagine ridiculing feminism and affirmative action in an environment in which their espousal is the only sure litmus test for political correctness, concluding that "Feminism is a disease of the rich: it is born of idleness, hence of leisure, hence of money"! Imagine investigating the contemporary welfare state and identifying benevolence as its besetting and unsustainable liability!

That is precisely what Stove does in the pages that follow. But wait a minute: Benevolence a liability? Isn't benevolence, on the contrary, a *good thing?* Let's think about that for a moment. Benevolence is a curious mental or characterological attribute. It is, as Stove observes, less a virtue than an emotion. To be benevolent means – what? To be disposed to relieve the misery and increase the happiness of others. Whether your benevolent attitude or action actually has that effect is beside the point. Yes, "benevolence, by the very meaning of the word, is a desire for the happiness, rather than the misery, of its object." But here's the rub:

the fact simply is that its actual effect is often the opposite of the intended one. The adult who had been hopelessly "spoiled" in childhood is the commonest kind of example; that is, someone who is unhappy in adult life because his parents were too successful, when he was a child, in protecting him from every source of *un*happiness.

It's not that benevolence is a bad thing per se. It's just that, like charity, it works best the more local are its aims. Enlarged, it becomes like that "telescopic philanthropy" Dickens attributes to Mrs. Jellyby in *Bleak House*. Her philanthropy is more ardent the more abstract and distant its objects. When it comes to her own family, she is hopeless.

The sad truth is that theoretical benevolence is compatible with any amount of practical indifference or even cruelty. You feel kindly toward others. That is what matters: your feelings. The *effects* of your benevolent feelings in the real world are secondary. Rousseau was a philosopher of benevolence. So was Karl Marx. Yet everywhere that Marx's ideas have been put into practice, the result has been universal immiseration. But his intention was the benevolent one of forging a more equitable society by abolishing private property and, to adopt a famous phrase from President Obama, by spreading the wealth around.

An absolute commitment to benevolence, like the road that is paved with good intentions, typically leads to an unprofitable destination. My epigraph from the great nineteenth-century English essayist Walter Bagehot underscores the point: it is a melancholy occupation, observed Bagehot, to ask whether the benevolence of mankind actually does more good than ill. It makes the purveyor of benevolence feel better – where by "better" I mean "more smug and self-righteous." But it is unclear whether the *objects* of benevolence are any better off.

Just so with the modern welfare state: a sterling incarnation of the sort of abstract benevolence Stove anatomizes. It doesn't matter that the welfare state actually creates more of the poverty and dependence it was instituted to abolish: the intentions behind it are benevolent. Which is one of the reasons it is so seductive. It flatters the vanity of those who espouse it even as it nourishes the egalitarian ambitions that have always been at the center of Enlightened thought. This is why Stove describes benevolence as "the heroin of the Enlightened." It is intoxicating, addictive, expensive, and ultimately ruinous.

The intoxicating effects of benevolence help to explain the growing appeal of politically correct attitudes about everything from "the environment" to the fate of the Third World. Why does the consistent failure of statist policies not disabuse their advocates of the statist agenda? One reason is that statist policies have the sanction of benevolence. They are "against poverty," "against war," "against oppression," "for the environment." And why shouldn't they be? Where else are the pleasures of smug self-righteousness to be had at so little cost?

The intoxicating effects of benevolence also help to explain why unanchored benevolence is inherently expansionist. The party of benevolence is always the party of big government. The imperatives of benevolence are intrinsically opposed to the pragmatism that underlies the allegiance to limited government.

Stove's argument is that the union of abstract benevolence,

which takes mankind as a whole for its object, with unbridled moralism is a toxic, misery-producing brew. "It is only the combination of these two elements," Stove observes in a powerful essay called "Why You Should Be a Conservative,"

> which is so powerful a cause of modern misery. Either element on its own is almost always comparatively harmless. A person who is convinced that he has a moral obligation to be benevolent, but who in fact ranks morality below fame (say), or ease; or again, a person who puts morality first, but is also convinced that the supreme moral obligation is, not to be benevolent, but to be holy (say), or wise, or creative: either of these people might turn out to be a scourge of his fellow humans, though in most cases he will not. But even at the worst, the misery which such a person causes will fall incomparably short of the misery caused by Lenin, or Stalin, or Mao, or Ho Chi Minh, or Kim Il-sung, or Pol Pot, or Castro: persons convinced both of the supremacy of benevolence among moral obligations, and of the supremacy of morality among all things. It is this combination which is infallibly and enormously destructive of human happiness.

Of course, as Stove goes on to note, this "lethal combination" is by no means peculiar to communists. It provides the emotional fuel for utopians from Robespierre to the politically correct bureaucrats who preside over more and more of life in Western societies today. They mean well. They seek to boost all mankind up to their own plane of enlightenment.

Foreword

Inequality outrages their sense of justice. They regard conventional habits of behavior as so many obstacles to be overcome on the path to perfection. They see tradition as the enemy of innovation, which they embrace as a lifeline to moral progress. They cannot encounter a wrong without seeking to right it. The idea that some evils may be ineradicable is anathema. The notion that the best is the enemy of the good, that many choices are to some extent choices among evils – such proverbial wisdom seems quaintly out of date. The result is a campaign to legislate virtue, to curtail eccentricity, to smother individuality, to barter truth for the current moral or political enthusiasm.

For centuries, political philosophers have understood that the lust for equality is the enemy of freedom. That species of benevolence underwrote the tragedy of communist tyranny. The rise of political correctness has redistributed that lust over a new roster of issues: not the proletariat, but the environment, not the struggling masses, but "reproductive freedom," gay rights, the welfare state, the Third World, diversity training, and an end to racism and xenophobia. It looks, in Marx's famous mot, like history repeating itself as farce. It would be a rash man, however, who made no provision for a reprise of tragedy.

Such attitudes are all but ubiquitous in modern democratic societies. Although of relatively recent vintage, they have spread rapidly. The triumph of this aspect of Enlightened thinking marked the moment when "the softening of human life became the great, almost the only, moral desideratum," Stove notes.

Foreword

The genius of Rousseau made the shedding of tears the hallmark of moral elevation: a thing which was, with good reason, without precedent in European life. Classes of people who had previously been only on the margin of the moral map, or off the map altogether — children, women, servants, the poor, prisoners, the insane, slaves — found themselves all at once at the center, and the object of a powerful outpouring of benevolence. Every earlier human landmark of moral authority, whether dating from antiquity or the Christian centuries, was buried under a tidal wave of benevolence. Leonidas and St. Anthony, Cato the Elder and Joan of Arc, Luther and Loyola, all met a common doom; and the new moral hero, to replace all these, who was he? Why, the *benevolent* man, "The Man of Feeling."

The modern welfare state is one result of the triumph of abstract benevolence. Its chief effects are to institutionalize dependence on the state while also assuring the steady growth of the bureaucracy charged with managing government largess. Both help to explain why the welfare state has proved so difficult to dismantle. The governments that support the welfare state, Stove points out,

> are elected by universal adult franchise; but an electorally decisive proportion of the voters — in some countries, approaching a quarter — either is employed by government or is dependent to a significant extent on some welfare program. In these circumstances it is

merely childish to expect the welfare state to be reduced, at least while there is universal suffrage. A government that did away with free education, for
example, or socialized medicine, simply could not be
re-elected. Indeed it would be lucky to see out its term
of office.

Is there an alternative? Stove quotes Thomas Malthus's
observation, from his famous *Essay on Population*, that "we are
indebted for all the noblest exertions of human genius, for
everything that distinguishes the civilized from the savage
state," to "the laws of property and marriage, and to the apparently narrow principle of self-interest which prompts each
individual to exert himself in bettering his condition." Stove
observes that Malthus's arguments for the genuinely beneficent
effects of "the apparently narrow principle of self-interest" are
truths that "cannot be too often repeated." But I am not sure he
truly acknowledges the power he discerns in them.

Indeed, my one serious quibble with Stove's argument in
this book concerns his fatalism, patent in this passage. It would
be "merely childish" to expect the welfare state to be reduced
only if you accepted that the beneficiaries of the welfare state
were incapable of understanding and taking effective action
against its enervating imperatives. Stove ends his book with
the image of a wise Indian in his canoe who finds himself
caught in a current that will ultimately propel him over Niagara Falls. For hours, he struggles manfully to escape the
current. Eventually, however, the futility of his efforts is in -
escapable. Then he "ships his paddle, lights his pipe, and folds
his arms," says Stove.

Foreword

In the circumstances, those are the actions of a rational man. Similarly, in my opinion, the world-current of Enlightened benevolence is now so strong, and we have been launched upon it for so many years, that we passed the point of no return a long time ago, and will, if we are rational, emulate the Indian in the story.

I write in November 2010. The United States has just had an election that many see as a remarkable, if still inchoate, push-back against that current of misplaced benevolence that has shackled us with the welfare state and all its depredations. The end is by no means certain. But the Indian in Stove's story would be foolish to stow his paddle when so many opportunities for escape were still opening up before him.

ROGER KIMBALL
Norwalk, Connecticut

INTRODUCTION

Counteracting the Efforts of the Good

Self-love resembles the instrument by which we perpetuate the species. It is necessary, it is dear to us, it gives us pleasure and it has to be concealed.
VOLTAIRE
A Philosophical Dictionary

The science of constructing a commonwealth, or renovating it, or reforming it, is, like every other experimental science, not to be taught a priori. Nor is it a short experience that can instruct us in that practical science.
EDMUND BURKE
Reflections on the Revolution in France

Tradition means giving votes to the most obscure of all classes, our ancestors. It is the democracy of the dead. Tradition refuses to submit to the small and arrogant oligarchy who merely happen to be walking about.
G. K. CHESTERTON
Orthodoxy

I did not ever want — no conservative should have wanted — the Russian empire to collapse as quickly *as it has done.*
DAVID STOVE
in correspondence

I

Introduction

DAVID STOVE is a confirming instance of the adage that philosophers are not much accustomed to attention until after they're dead. During his lifetime, Stove was little known outside his native Australia. To be sure, his name was recognized at universities around the world both as a Hume scholar and as a philosopher of science, but among members of the broader international public he was all but unknown. This began to change some years after his death with the American publication of several collections of his less technical papers. The current book marks the release of the last of Stove's major essays that remained unpublished at the time of his death.

Like John Stuart Mill's *On Liberty* and Friedrich Hayek's *The Road to Serfdom*, Stove's essay on benevolence takes as its main focus the relationship between authority and the individual. But while Mill and Hayek are content to defend the classic liberal imperative, Stove goes a step further, asking whether liberalism and conservatism are in any important sense compatible. His answer is that they are, that conservative institutions flourish most when individual liberty is at its maximum and state authority is at its minimum. According to Stove, when people are free to live their lives as they see fit, they naturally choose to enter into relationships with one another that allow families, friendships, businesses and other non-governmental institutions to flourish. Far from being troubled by the apparently paradoxical observation that conservatism thrives in nations founded on liberal principles, Stove sees this as a natural and healthy consequence of liberalism. As the nineteenth-century economist Thomas Malthus put it, once people are left to their own devices, "the apparently narrow principle of self-interest which prompts each individual to exert himself in bettering his condition" causes us to adopt not just the age-old "laws of property and marriage," but other conservative principles and institutions as well.[1]

For many, this connection between liberalism and conservatism has not been immediately apparent. Hayek, for example, famously argued that the two traditions are fundamentally at odds with one another. In his 1960 essay "Why I Am Not a Conservative" he tells us that although liberalism and conservatism often find common cause, they are in an important sense incompatible:

> Since the development during the last decades has been generally in a socialist direction, it may seem that both conservatives and liberals have been mainly intent on retarding that movement. . . . But the main point about liberalism is that it wants to go elsewhere, not stand still. . . . Liberalism is not averse to evolution and change; and where spontaneous change has been smothered by government control, it wants a great deal of change of policy. So far as much of current government action is concerned, there is in the present world very little reason for the liberal to wish to preserve things as they are. It would seem to the liberal, indeed, that what is most urgently needed in most parts of the world is a thorough sweeping-away of the obstacles to free growth.[2]

Introduction

Hayek's core argument is this: Liberalism* requires the active defense of individual liberty. In contrast, conservatism requires only an opposition to dramatic change. In nations in which liberty is already at its maximum, conservatives and liberals will both want to preserve the status quo. But in nations in which state authority significantly hampers or limits individual liberty, liberals and conservatives will have dramatically different goals. The liberal will want to advance the cause of individual freedom. The conservative will want to protect the system of government currently in place, regardless of its strengths or weaknesses.

The result, says Hayek, is that liberalism and conservatism are distinguishable on at least five grounds. First, conservatives have "no goal of their own."[3] Being merely reactionary, they are opposed to change regardless of its merits. Conservatism by its very nature "cannot offer an alternative to the direction in which we are moving. It may succeed by its resistance to current tendencies in slowing down undesirable developments, but, since it does not indicate another direction, it cannot prevent their continuance."[4]

Second, conservatives have an unjustified fear of progress. In contrast to liberalism, which "is based on courage and confidence, on a preparedness to let change run its course even if we cannot predict where it will lead,"[5] conservatism is based on "a fear of change, a timid distrust of the new."[6] This timid distrust of the new is often connected to a kind of anti-

---

* Or what is also sometimes referred to as "traditional liberalism," "classical liberalism," or "libertarianism." See Friedrich A. Hayek, "Why I Am Not a Conservative" (1960), in *The Constitution of Liberty* (South Bend, Ind.: Gateway Editions, 1972), pp. 407ff.

intellectualism: "Conservatives feel instinctively that it is new ideas more than anything else that cause change."[7] As a result, conservatism has a "propensity to reject well-substantiated new knowledge because it dislikes some of the consequences which seem to follow from it."[8] Underlying this fear of new ideas is the fact that conservatism "has no distinctive principles of its own to oppose to them; and, by its distrust of theory and its lack of imagination concerning anything except that which experience has already proved, it deprives itself of the weapons needed in the struggle of ideas."[9]

Third, conservatives have an undue fondness for authority. When it is in their interest, they "are inclined to use the powers of government to prevent change."[10] According to Hayek, the conservative "feels safe and content only if he is assured that some higher wisdom watches and supervises change, only if he knows that some authority is charged with keeping the change 'orderly.'"[11] Once again, this is in direct contrast to liberalism, a theory of human development in which change is seen as inevitable and healthy: "It is, indeed, part of the liberal attitude to assume that, especially in the economic field, the self-regulating forces of the market will somehow bring about the required adjustments to new conditions, although no one can foretell how they will do this in a particular instance."[12] Put in other words, "it can probably be said that the conservative does not object to coercion or arbitrary power so long as it is used for what he regards as the right purposes. . . . Like the socialist, he is less concerned with the problem of how the powers of government should be limited than with that of who wields them; and like the socialist, he regards himself as entitled to force the value he holds on other people."[13]

Fourth, conservatives have a "lack of understanding of economic forces."[14] Conservatives not only advocate protectionism and are opposed to internationalism, they often lack even a basic understanding of how economic growth is related to the need for liberty and to the "spontaneous forces on which a policy of freedom relies."[15]

Finally, conservatism is unprincipled. Put another way, conservatism lacks an underlying political philosophy. As a result, conservatism is not so much an alternative to either liberalism or socialism, but simply a rule of action, and although a rule of action may turn out to be helpful in specific circumstances, it hardly can run proxy for a full-fledged theory of human nature and political responsibility: "Though *quieta non movere* ['let sleeping dogs lie'] may at times be a wise maxim for the statesman, it cannot satisfy the political philosopher. He may wish policy to proceed gingerly and not before public opinion is prepared to support it, but he cannot accept arrangements merely because current opinion sanctions them."[16] Of course, Hayek is quick to point out that the charge of being unprincipled is not the same as the charge of being unethical: "When I say that the conservative lacks principles, I do not mean to suggest that he lacks moral conviction. The typical conservative is indeed usually a man of very strong moral convictions."[17] Instead, being unprincipled means only that conservatism fails to be concerned with the kinds of general guiding principles capable of giving a uniform explanation of all political action. "In this sense," says Hayek, "I doubt whether there can be such a thing as a conservative political philosophy. Conservatism may often be a useful practical maxim, but it does not give us any guiding principles which can influence long-range developments."[18]

What are we to make of these five criticisms? Partly the modern conservative will want to point out that in the half century since Hayek wrote, conservatism has changed a great deal, not least as a result of Hayek's own writings. To see this, we need only think of how influential Hayek has been in convincing conservatives to adopt policies favoring the free market. Perhaps more than any other author, it is because of Hayek that traditional liberals and modern conservatives have made common cause with regard to the economy. But what will the conservative say in response to Hayek's other four criticisms? What will the conservative say in response to the suggestion that conservatives have no goal of their own, that they have a fear of progress and a fondness for authority, and that conservatism lacks an underlying political philosophy?

* * *

David Stove's essay on benevolence was written during a year of optimism.* The year 1989 was not only the two-hundredth anniversary of the French Revolution, it was also the year the fall of the Berlin Wall unexpectedly signalled an end to the Cold War. Just as the storming of the Bastille had initiated a turning away from the age of absolutism, the fall of the Berlin Wall initiated a turning away from the age of communism. Even so, Stove was hesitant to join in the general

---

* It is not possible to date the essay exactly. Even so, from internal references it is possible to conclude that most if not all of it was written between February and October 1989.

celebrations. A supporter of neither the divine right of kings nor twentieth-century communism, he remained concerned not just about society's rapid rate of social change, but also about the continued influence of socialism.

For Stove, the best argument for conservatism comes from the well-established empirical fact that because we are fallible beings, our actions, both individually and collectively, almost always have unforeseen and unwelcome consequences whose disadvantages often outweigh their benefits. "There are a million examples one could give," says Stove,

> drawn from the effects of "welfare" legislation on societies like ours, from the effects of western technology on primitive societies, and so on. But I will go at once to the biggest and most obvious example of all: twentieth-century communism. This is an evil so appalling that some ignorant or superstitious people believe that its psychological roots can only lie in Satanism, or even in Satan himself. But in sober fact it is beyond question that the psychological root of twentieth-century communism is benevolence. Lenin, Stalin, and the rest, would not have done what they did, but for the fact that they began by wishing the human race well. Communists differ, of course, from other Friends of Humanity, in certain beliefs that they have about the conditions necessary for achieving human happiness. But the emotional fuel of communism has always been the same as the emotional *fuel* of all utopianisms: the passionate wish to abolish or alleviate human misery.[19]

Introduction

Put another way, good intentions alone are never enough to justify revolutionary social change. Given the intricacy of human society, it is a practical certainty that sweeping, revolutionary reform will have unanticipated results: results that will turn out to be worse than the hardship the reform is intended to eliminate. If reforms are to be made, they need to be well tested, local in scope and as non-coercive as possible. As Stove puts it,

> innovators-for-the-worse have always been far *more* numerous than innovators-for-the-better: they always *must* be so. Consider the practical side first. Do you understand television sets well enough to be able to repair a non-functioning one or to improve a malfunctioning one? Probably not: very few do. And if you, being one of the great majority, nevertheless do set out to repair or improve a TV set, it is a million to one, because of the complexity of the thing, that you will make it worse if you change it at all. Now human societies, at least ones as large and rich as ours, are incomparably more complex than TV sets, and in fact no one understands them well enough to repair or improve them. Whatever some people may claim, there are no society repairmen, as there are TV repairmen. So if anyone gets to try out in practice his new idea for repairing or improving our society, it is something like billions to one that he will actually make things worse if he changes them at all. Of course it is possible that he will make things better, but that is trivially true: it is possible, after all, that a furious kick will repair your ailing TV set.[20]

Introduction

It follows that large-scale social change needs to be made slowly and cautiously, and that the burden of proof in evaluating new political proposals will lie with the advocate of reform, not with the opponent. Conservatism thus finds itself universally opposed to sweeping, revolutionary change. It also finds itself in agreement with the traditional liberal's claim that individual choices are a far more reliable basis of social policy than top-down government decisions. As Mill tells us,

> the great majority of things are worse done by the intervention of government, than the individuals most interested in the matter would do them, or cause them to be done, if left to themselves. The grounds of this truth are expressed with tolerable exactness in the popular dictum, that people understand their own business and their own interests better, and care for them more, than the government does, or can be expected to do. This maxim holds true throughout the greatest part of the business of life, and wherever it is true we ought to condemn every kind of government intervention that conflicts with it.[21]

In short, Stove's law of unforeseen consequences and Mill's law of individual responsibility together help form something of a bridge between traditional conservatism and traditional liberalism. By minimizing the role of government we maximize our protection against inevitable political calamity. By maximizing individual responsibility we minimize the effect of unforeseen harmful consequences.

* * *

Introduction

Underlying Stove's law of unforeseen consequences and Mill's law of individual responsibility is a conservative theory of human nature. To see this, one need only remember that the actual essence of conservatism is not, as Hayek suggests, simple opposition to far-reaching change. To think so is to confuse consequence with cause. Instead, the essence of conservatism is the conviction that the human situation is characterized both by inescapable fallibility and by erratic, inconsistent preferences. Errors in judgment regularly lead us astray. Inconsistent wants inevitably result in our profound dissatisfaction with the state of the world. As Stove puts it,

> We are hopelessly beset by conflicting desires. Like Charles V, we want both the pleasures of privacy and the pleasures of power, no matter how improbable or impossible their combination may be. Like Bing Crosby and Louis Armstrong, we want both a quiet fishing-spot, and the money we cannot make there.
>
> This is constantly illustrated even in our little suburban lives. Professor W retires, promising to write the important book which, he says, the burdens of teaching and administration have for twenty years prevented him from writing. In fact, of course, he had actively sought those burdens (and more), and he will never write that book. He clears his desk at home for action, but nothing happens. The paper remains blank, and he is beginning to panic, when – thank God! – the phone rings. Would he agree to serve on the citizens' committee for X? Or to act as external examiner for Y? Or to come as a visiting lecturer to Z? He closes with every

offer. It is not that he does not really want to write that
book; but he wants, even more, to do other things
which are in fact incompatible with writing it. . . .

The fact is that, as Hume said in *The Natural History of Religion*, "it is not possible for us, by our most
chimerical wishes, to form the idea of a station or situation altogether desirable." The reason is that we
desire incompatible things. Even if every other cause
of human misery were removed, and even if only a
single person were in question, that person's desires,
being inconsistent, would still be incapable of satisfaction. Remold this sorry scheme of things exactly to
your heart's desires: then even if, by some miracle,
those desires were compatible with one another, you
would sooner or later be bored with the result. In
other words, the universal human hankering for novelty would, at some stage, intervene and unsettle all.[22]

The essence of conservatism is thus not mere opposition
to change. Instead, it is the conviction that we are all subject
to competing internal tensions,* tensions that may be mitigated but never completely eliminated by the political and
social structures in which we live. Put another way, the goal of
the conservative is not to avoid change but to enable change
to be made safely, or at least as safely as possible. Given our
inevitable shortcomings, and the inevitable human shortcomings of our political leaders, the conservative encourages a

---

* In Christian theology, this is often referred to as the doctrine of original
sin.

variety of social institutions – families, businesses, religious organizations, elected governments, NGOs – to flourish. By refusing to allow power to be concentrated in any single institution, conservatism diversifies risk, thereby cushioning society from the inevitable failure of any one institution.

Hayek is thus wrong on at least three counts. He is wrong to think that conservatism has no underlying political philosophy. He is wrong to think that conservatives have no positive goal of their own.* And he is wrong to think that conservatives have a special fondness for authority. In other words, he is wrong to think that "Like the socialist, [the conservative] is less concerned with the problem of how the powers of government should be limited than with that of who wields them."[23] On this point especially, the conservative shares a great deal with the traditional liberal.† The only significant difference is that while the liberal believes that the powers of government need to be limited by ensuring that each individual is sovereign within his own domain, the conservative recognizes that no man is an island, and that it is natural and right for individuals, once left to their

---

* Of course there is a sense in which it is true that conservatives have no positive "goal of their own," since the conservative, like the liberal, wants such goals to be largely a function of individual choice. But because this is a view held in common between liberals and conservatives, it can hardly be raised by the liberal as a criticism against the conservative.

† Numerous other points of agreement appear as well. For example, consider the following key comment by Hayek: "What I have described as the liberal position shares with conservatism a distrust of reason to the extent that the liberal is very much aware that we do not know all the answers and that he is not sure that the answers he has are certainly the right ones or even that we can find all the answers." Hayek, "Why I Am Not a Conservative," p. 406.

own devices, to want to join together to form a variety of non-governmental institutions, many of which, although voluntarily formed, have significant power and influence over their members' lives. This diversity of institutions not only allows individuals to benefit from each other's varying abilities, it helps protect us from our unavoidable individual shortcomings.

Even so, Hayek is right when he suggests that it is on the issue of change that the liberal and the conservative disagree. While the liberal sees change as inevitable and healthy, the conservative sees change as fraught with danger.

Of course this overstates the point slightly. For the conservative, as for the liberal, *individual* change is often perfectly agreeable. Just as we often shun change simply because we prefer the routine and the familiar, we also often welcome change, if for no other reason than that we simply enjoy the new. And as Mill reminds us, "people understand their own business and their own interests better, and care for them more, than the government does, or can be expected to do." With regard to all such decisions, or with regard to what Hayek calls "spontaneous change," the individual is king.

In contrast, when it comes to extensive, top-down, revolutionary change, Hayek is right to think that the conservative has "a fear of change, a timid distrust of the new." As a result, just as the liberal is committed to the maximization of individual freedom, the conservative is committed to the diversification of political power among a wide range of social institutions, believing that it is only by encouraging this diversification that we can protect ourselves from the unintended and unwelcome consequences of revolutionary action. If a slogan is needed, it is this: Benevolence alone is never enough. Human failure, at some level, is inescapable. Good intentions alone inevitably lead to misery. What is needed is a diversified society, a society structured in such a way as to protect us from our own weaknesses. What is needed is restrictions on the growth of institutions that threaten to become too large and too influential, and that are likely to obtain a monopoly on power. What is needed is restrictions on the growth of government.

* * *

In preparing the manuscript, I have understood it to be an editor's prerogative, in consultation with the author's literary executor, to alter the occasional word or phrase that had not received final editing at the time of the author's death. Throughout the essay, punctuation has also been standardized. In all cases the changes have been modest and have served either to clarify the author's intent or to improve the writing stylistically. Nowhere has the substance of the essay been changed or abbreviated, and nowhere, I hope, has the author's clear, honest prose been compromised.

In the case of references, I have taken the liberty of standardizing the author's style of citation throughout. I have also added a series of editor's footnotes to supplement the author's original source notes. In consultation with the publisher, the original title (*That Monstrous Steep, Niagara,* or *Happiness, Benevolence, and Private Property*) has been changed. In all of these respects, the editing has been no more intrusive than the kinds of editorial changes to which

Introduction

Stove gave consent, at times grudgingly, during his lifetime.

For readers interested in the sources of the author's two opening epigraphs, the Gorky quotation can be found in Edmund Wilson's *To the Finland Station* (New York: Harcourt, Brace & Co., 1940), pp. 450–51. Both sets of ellipsis points appear in the original. The second quotation appears in William Rathbone Greg's *Enigmas of Life*, 15th ed. (London: Trübner & Co., 1883), p. 159. For readers interested in the sources of the opening epigraphs to this Introduction, the Voltaire quotation appears in *Dictionnaire philosophique, portatif, nouvelle édition* (London, 1765), under "Amour-propre," p. 20; the Burke quotation appears in *Reflections on the Revolution in France* (London: J. Dodsley, 1790), p. 90; the Chesterton quotation appears in *Orthodoxy* (New York: Dodd, Mead and Co., 1959), p. 85; and the Stove quotation appears in a letter written on December 30, 1991.

ANDREW IRVINE
Vancouver, British Columbia

WHAT'S WRONG WITH BENEVOLENCE

I have never met in Russia, the country where the in-evitability of suffering is preached as the general road to salvation, nor have I ever known of any man anywhere, who hated, despised, and loathed all unhappiness, grief, and suffering so deeply and strongly as Lenin did. . . . He was particularly great, in my opinion, precisely because `.` . . of his burning faith that suffering was not an essential and unavoidable part of life, but an abomination that people ought to and could sweep away.
MAXIM GORKY, quoted in Edmund Wilson,
To the Finland Station

. . . in this world, a large part of the business of the wise is to counteract the efforts of the good.
WILLIAM RATHBONE GREG
Enigmas of Life

HOMER SAYS that humans are the unhappiest of all crea-
tures.[1] Even if he was mistaken about the comparative happiness of other species, human unhappiness is certainly far
greater than any words adequately can express. Why are we
so unhappy?

According to Thomas Malthus,* the main causes of
human unhappiness are war, famine, and pestilence. Of
course by "famine" he meant poverty in general, and by
"pestilence" disease in general. But even on that understanding, Malthus's opinion is still so astoundingly false that it
takes one's breath away. Consider, for example, the millions
of people who nowadays consult psychiatrists because they
are unhappy. Not one in a thousand of them is unhappy
because of war or poverty. Not one in twenty of them is
unhappy because of any physical disease; and as for the idea
of "mental disease," who would trust *that* frail notion to

* Thomas Robert Malthus was born in Surrey in 1766. He was ordained
in 1797. A year later he anonymously published his *Essay on the Principle
of Population as It Affects the Future Improvement of Society*. Subsequently
he was appointed professor of political economy at the East India Col-
lege, Haileybury. He went on to become one of Britain's most influential
nineteenth-century economists. He died in 1834. – Ed.

account for even a quarter of the unfortunates who today fill psychiatrists' waiting rooms?

Further, even if the causes to which Malthus ascribed human misery had not been ridiculously inadequate, they would still have been ridiculously few. The causes of our misery are inexhaustibly various, and so numerous as to include almost everything. This woman's life is embittered by childlessness; that woman's life is embittered by her children. Some men are unhappy because they have never shed their own or an enemy's blood in war; many more are unhappy because they have. Poverty is, indeed, a common cause of unhappiness; but there is also profound truth in the old story of King Midas.

Is there, in fact, anything that has *not* been a source of affliction to many people? It might be supposed that health, and normal bodily functioning, constitute such an exception. Yet in countless instances, devotees of various religions have blinded or castrated or otherwise injured themselves because the normal functioning of their bodies, eyes, or genitals was a torment to them.

Two of the causes of misery which Malthus mentions are external ones: war and poverty. Elsewhere* I have referred to the "externalism" to which all Enlightenment thinkers subscribed: namely their belief that human beings are made what they are by external influences such as education, or the form of government or distribution of wealth prevailing around

---

* For example, see D. C. Stove, "The Bateson Fact, or One in a Million," in D. C. Stove, *On Enlightenment* (New Brunswick, N.J., and London: Transaction Publishers, 2003), p. 53. Also see D. C. Stove, "The Diabolical Place: A Secret of the Enlightenment," *Encounter*, 74:4 (May 1990), pp. 14–15, reprinted in D. C. Stove, *On Enlightenment*, pp. 106–7. – Ed.

them. Malthus expressly and effectively challenged that belief, yet we have only to look at his own list of the main causes of unhappiness to see that he himself was by no means free from its influence. To suppose that, in the absence of war and poverty, human misery would be deprived of two-thirds of its sources implies a remarkable ability to underestimate the inner sources of our misery.

Suppose you wanted to make a population of pigeons or leopards, say, permanently happier than they ever have been before. How might you do this if you are not allowed to change the pigeons or leopards themselves, but only their external circumstances? This problem is worth considering, because it must be more easily soluble than the corresponding problem in the human case. Yet even a little reflection will suffice to show how intractable the problem is, even in this easier case. Quite apart from such external constraints as your own limited resources, there are reasons, inherent in pigeons or leopards themselves, which will prevent the realization of your pigeon- or leopard-utopia.

One reason is the Malthusian one: that pigeons or leopards, once they are happier than they ever have been before, will not remain so for long, because they will then multiply so rapidly that the misery due to hunger will soon resume its old dominion over them. Another reason is this: one of the necessary conditions of happiness, if you are a leopard, is *not* to have human beings superintending your life. Leopards are like many human populations who once were subjected to foreign rule, but are so no longer: they prefer even the worst government by their own kind to even the best government by any other.

It should go without saying that *Homo sapiens* is far more "plastic" to external influences than pigeons or leopards. Yet consider human beings even when they are most susceptible to external influence: when they are infants or young children, and are governed by parents or teachers every hour of their waking lives. Have parents or teachers always found this human material to be putty in their hands? Some of the Enlightened, Helvéticus for example, did not shrink from answering yes to this question. But the *actual* experience of parents or teachers in all ages is, of course, emphatically the opposite: that, in countless instances, even infant human nature has proved to be as resistant as marble to some, or all, of the influences which adults bring to bear upon it. So very far, then, are external circumstances from being decisive, even when every advantage is on their side.

BUT EVEN among external causes of unhappiness, Malthus omits to mention one, which hardly anyone else ever mentions either, although it has been as great a source of unhappiness as war or poverty, at least in recent centuries. In the twentieth century in particular, it has even been the *cause* of most of our wars and famines. I mean *benevolence*.

There is a slight air of paradox in calling benevolence a cause of unhappiness. Yet there should not be, because everyone knows of many instances in which it is so. Of course benevolence, by the very meaning of the word, is a desire for the happiness, rather than the misery, of its object; but the fact simply is that its actual effect is often the opposite of the intended one. The adult who had been hopelessly "spoiled" in childhood is the commonest kind of example; that is, someone who is unhappy in adult life because his parents were too successful, when he was a child, in protecting him from every source of *un*happiness.

A larger-scale example of benevolence causing misery is the following one, which is only slightly idealized. A primitive people, much reduced in numbers, is threatened with absolute extinction by a certain disease. Benevolence prompts us to save them by bringing modern medicine to bear on the case. The disease is defeated; but, as a result, the population explodes and famine threatens. Benevolence compels us to supply food and to introduce contraception in order to limit population; but contraception revolutionizes personal morality and the family structure, and in fifteen years' time we find that we have dismantled yet another primitive culture. Will anyone deny that there has been more than one instance of this sort, of misery caused by benevolence?

But of all the examples of benevolence causing misery, easily the most important is twentieth-century communism. This is an evil so appalling that some ignorant or superstitious people believe that its psychological roots can only lie in Satanism, or even in Satan himself. But in sober fact it is quite certain that the psychological root of communism is benevolence. Lenin, Stalin, and the rest would not have done what they did, but for the fact that they were determined to bring about the future happiness of the human race. Communists differ from other utopians, of course, in certain beliefs they have about the conditions which are necessary for achieving universal happiness; but the emotional *fuel* of communism is, and always has been, exactly the same as the emotional fuel of every other utopianism: the passionate desire to alleviate or abolish misery. Yet everyone knows what the *actual* effects of communism are: an unprecedented degree and extent of misery wherever the communists have triumphed; and wherever they are still resisted by force, inextinguishable war and in many cases famine as well.

Since benevolence is sometimes, yet obviously not always, productive of misery, what is it that makes the difference between the two outcomes? How is one to tell in advance the dangerous kind of benevolence from the other? This question is not easy to answer; but there are certain features which, when they are all present at once, are a very strong indication of the dangerous kind.

One of these features is *universality*. Benign or harmless benevolence is typically local in its objects, or confined to a special class of people (the sick, for example); whereas dangerous benevolence typically has for its object all present and future human beings. A second warning feature is *disinterestedness*. When a Condorcet, a Bentham, or a Marx plans for universal happiness, there is "nothing in it" (as we say) for Condorcet, Bentham, or Marx himself. Whereas, of course, when a father plans his child's happiness, or a teacher his pupil's, or a friend his friend's, there is something in it, should the plan succeed, for the father, teacher, or friend: there is the increased affection of the child, the gratitude of the pupil, strengthened friendship with the friend. The third warning sign of dangerous benevolence is *externality*. That is, it is proposed to bring about the happiness of others, not by changing them, but by changing their circumstances: by giving them money, for example, or better surroundings, or legal rights which they did not have before.

Even where benevolence is universal, disinterested, and external, it need not be dangerous. It might happen, for example, that the external means which are disinterestedly proposed for making everyone happy are so obviously unlikely to achieve this end that the proposal cannot muster popular support. Still, where benevolence does combine the three features I have mentioned, it needs only the additional

element of popularity in order to be extremely dangerous;
just as a firearm, loaded and "at the ready," needs only pressure on the trigger to fire. This much can be read straight off
the record of human history; or, at least, off the record of
human history of the last few centuries.

III

THE QUALIFICATION, "of the last few centuries," is necessary, because benevolence of the kind in question – the universal, disinterested, and external kind – is a thing only of yesterday in human history. It was in fact invented, and elevated into our highest virtue, by the Enlightenment.*

In earlier times, virtues akin to such benevolence had often been ranked high. The munificence of a Renaissance prince, for example, or of a Roman patron in the late republic; the gentleness of a perfect knight, according to Froissart or Malory; the humanity which victorious generals, in all ages, have occasionally displayed towards their defeated enemies.

---

* Unlike the seventeenth-century Age of Reason (in which reason was proclaimed as the fundamental source of both scientific understanding and social authority), the eighteenth-century Age of Enlightenment generally involved a dramatic critical questioning of traditional institutions, customs, and morals. Although there is little agreement about precise dates, there is wide consensus about the Enlightenment's underlying theory. As Stove puts it, "It was always obvious enough what the main axioms of the Enlightenment were. They were secularism, egalitarianism, and the utilitarian axiom, that the test of morality is the greatest happiness of the greatest number." The critical questioning associated with the Enlightenment led in turn to the Age of Revolution. See D. C. Stove, "The Diabolical Place: A Secret of the Enlightenment," in *On Enlightenment*, p. 93. – Ed.

But, of course, all of these things are very different from the benevolence – the "enlarged" benevolence, as they used to say – of the Enlightenment.

That the best quality a human being can have is a strong disposition to maximize the happiness of humans – of humans without restriction, and of humans as we actually find them to be – was an Enlightenment belief, however, and a belief the novelty of which it is scarcely possible to exaggerate. It may sound like a truism to the vulgar now, but that counts as nothing. It was utterly foreign, and equally foreign, to Homer and to Shakespeare, to Plato and Aquinas, to Pericles, Calvin, and Charles V. Scarcely a single human being before about 1720 ever so much as dreamed of ranking benevolence above, or even alongside, such virtues as sanctity, or courage, or chastity, or loyalty, or patriotism, or justice.

Among the later Stoic philosophers, there are partial anticipations of the Enlightenment's favorite virtue, but easily the closest earlier approach to it is to be found in that charity by which Christians, in their first two centuries, often amazed their contemporaries. This did not last very long, even among Christians, and certainly it never became the ruling morality of the age. By the fourth century A D, the ferocity of Christians towards one another, both in their doctrinal disputes and in their competition for wealthy bishoprics, was as proverbial as their love of one another had been earlier. But while it did last, Christian charity was not confined (as one might easily suppose it would have been) to other Christians. It was sometimes exercised, for example, in raising money to ransom non-Christian prisoners of war, as well as Christian ones.[2] Their benevolence appears to have been genuinely universal; nor is there any reason to doubt that it was disinterested as well.

But it was emphatically not external. To Christians of (say) 130 AD, the idea that the maximum of human happiness requires only better housing, education, laws, and the like would have seemed as perfectly ridiculous as ... as it really is. They did more than anyone had ever done before to relieve the misery of the homeless, the sick, the "despised and rejected."* But *happiness* was something different altogether. So far as they acknowledged the possibility of it at all on earth – at any rate until the "second coming" – they held that it depended, not on cheap rents or free false teeth from the National Health Service, but on a mysterious, and in any case entirely inward, process of conversion. This is a view of human happiness which, despite the absurd metaphysics in which it is embedded, is a great deal more realistic than that of most Christians of the present day; especially of those countless Christian priests who now expect human happiness to be installed by guerrilla war and Kalashnikov rifles.

How did the Enlightenment erect benevolence into our highest virtue? It did so partly by the elimination of rival candidates. It laughed or shamed almost every other virtue out of court. The "monkish virtues," as it called such things as humility, chastity, and obedience, were the principal victims. But the military virtues (such as courage), the feudal virtues (such as loyalty), the patriarchal virtues, the feminine virtues, and others all suffered the same fate. Likewise the idea of an individual's moral responsibilities being assigned to him by his birth: the idea of "my station and its duties."†

* Cf. Isaiah 53:3. – Ed.

† Originally found in the Church of England's *Book of Common Prayer*, the phrase was popularized by F. H. Bradley in his essay "My Station and Its Duties," in *Ethical Studies* (London: Oxford University Press, 1876), pp. 145–92. – Ed.

Benevolence won, then, partly by the default of rival virtues.

But there was also a positive process at work, pushing the virtue of benevolence into ever-greater prominence. Somewhere between about 1720 and 1750, a conviction stole over the minds of educated men that human life had always before been *needlessly hard*. It seemed to have been discovered for the first time that there was *room* for happiness in human life, where the urgencies of subsistence, of religion, of war, and of government had always previously prevented this possibility from being noticed. I cannot explain this great and sudden revolution in feeling. The enormous decline of religion at this time, combined with the memory of the religious wars which had so recently harrowed England, France, and Germany, must have played some part in it. But whatever may be its explanation, this revolution in feeling was a fact. David Hume, as well as sharing in it, remarked upon it in print at the time. In 1751 he wrote of the enthusiasm which had prevailed "in this kingdom ... of late years ... among men in *active* life with regard to *public spirit*, and among those in *speculative* with regard to *benevolence*."[3] Hume acknowledges that this enthusiasm was in many instances pretended rather than real; but he also insists that it often was real, and that it was, in any case, new. He does not, however, suggest any explanation of it.

Suddenly, the *softening* of human life became the great, almost the only, moral desideratum. The genius of Rousseau made the shedding of tears the hallmark of moral elevation: a thing which was, with good reason, without precedent in European life. Classes of people who had previously been only on the margin of the moral map, or off the map altogether – children, women, servants, the poor, prisoners, the insane, slaves – found themselves all at once at the center, and the object of a powerful outpouring of benevolence. Every earlier human landmark of moral authority, whether dating from antiquity or the Christian centuries, was buried under a tidal wave of benevolence. Leonidas and St. Anthony, Cato the Elder and Joan of Arc, Luther and Loyola, all met a common doom; and the new moral hero, to replace all these, who was he? Why, the benevolent man, "The Man of Feeling."

Henry Mackenzie's novel of that name was published in 1771, and its impact was such that the book was soon compared to Rousseau's *Nouvelle Héloïse* (1761). Mackenzie was for decades a central figure of the Scottish Enlightenment: the friend of Hume and William Robertson, a founding member of the Royal Society of Edinburgh, etc. But he also, like a prudent Scot, hedged his bets. He edited a depreciatory biography of Thomas Paine and wrote a second novel, *Julia de Roubigné* (1777), the theme of which was the harm that excessive benevolence can cause. But even *The Man of Feeling* had represented a somewhat inactive, local, and unprincipled benevolence: its affinities are with Sterne and Addison, rather than with the Friends of Humanity.

William Godwin provides a far more representative – because far more extravagant – specimen of the Enlightenment's apotheosis of the benevolent man. His words are much too long to be quoted, but can be fairly summarized as follows: If you are perfectly benevolent, Godwin says, you will be perfectly virtuous. If you are perfectly virtuous, you will be perfectly cheerful. You will then diffuse cheerfulness, virtue, and benevolence to all those around you. You will also, by being perfectly cheerful, be perfectly healthy: you will neither sicken, nor age, nor die.[4]

This all comes a little oddly from a notorious parasite who exhausted, as far as he could, the benevolence, or at any rate the purse, of everyone he came in contact with. But even apart from that, was a more superficial optimism ever conceived? It reminds one of nothing on earth, except perhaps the "Christian Science" of Mary Baker Eddy, or the advertising of some present-day "health clinics." It is painful to compare such brainless stuff with the sobriety of ethical thought in antiquity, especially among the later Stoics. If Godwin could have spent a week sharing the responsibilities of Marcus Aurelius, or even of Seneca, it might have imparted an improving touch of reality to his speculations. But of course this benevolence craze did not start or end with Godwin. He had absorbed it from such people as d'Holbach, Holcroft, and Condorcet, and he in turn imparted it to thousands. Most momentously, he imparted it to his disciple, Robert Owen, the father of British socialism.

Utilitarianism, as I have said elsewhere,* was an axiom of the Enlightenment. The Enlightenment measured the morality both of actions and of persons by their tendency to maximize the happiness of the greatest number of people. Its elevation of benevolence into the highest virtue was, therefore, an inevitable theorem.

---

* For example, see D. C. Stove, "The Diabolical Place: A Secret of the Enlightenment," in *On Enlightenment*, p. 93. – Ed.

BUT HAPPINESS was not the only ultimate moral value of the Enlightenment. There was another one, and one, perhaps, not always reconcilable with happiness: *equality*.

Equality as a moral value is, of course, something quite distinct from the egalitarianism which was also an axiom of the Enlightenment. *That* was the belief that human beings are *naturally* equal. What I am here speaking of is the conviction that every privilege, advantage, or superiority of one human being over another is *morally* wrong.

From this axiom, many important Enlightenment theorems obviously flow: for example, an enmity to kings, and to parents. But another and even more important theorem flows from this same axiom: communism, or an enmity to private property. This has often not been recognized as an Enlightenment theorem at all; yet its derivation is very obvious. For what inequality is more cruel, more glaring, or more arbitrary than inequality of property? What inequality brings so many other inequalities in its train? There ought *always*, therefore, to be equality of property, and there is only one way of ensuring *permanent* equality of property: community of property.

The same conclusion follows equally easily from the

greatest-happiness axiom. For no lesson of experience is more certain than that superior private wealth will always be principally used to maximize the happiness, not of the greatest number, but of the fortunate few.

It is very widely believed that the Enlightenment was an ideological expression of *bourgeois* economic interests. This belief originated with Marx and it is, accordingly, an article of faith among his followers; but it has also slowly become common among non-Marxist and even anti-Marxist thinkers. Nevertheless, it is false and, indeed, almost the exact opposite of the truth. The institution of private property never had, among the Enlightened, a single unqualified friend; only enemies of different degrees of intransigence and consistency. It could not have been otherwise: the derivation of communism, whether from the equality axiom or from the greatest-happiness axiom, was obvious and irresistible. *It still is.*

Communism was not, as contraception was, a secret theorem of the Enlightenment;* but it gradually became a semi-secret one. At first it was not a secret at all: unqualified condemnations of private property were common enough. Among the contemporaries of Rousseau, such minor Enlightenment figures as Morelly and Mably were avowed communists.[5] The famous slogan *"La propriété, c'est le vol"* – property is theft – was first coined, not by Proudhon in 1840, but by one Brissot de Warville some time before 1789.[6] Robert Wallace, who corresponded with Hume about population and who was one of Malthus's acknowledged influ-

---

* For additional discussion see D. C. Stove, "The Diabolical Place: A Secret of the Enlightenment," in *On Enlightenment*, pp. 93–110. – Ed.

ences, recommended the abolition of private property in his *Various Prospects of Mankind, Nature, and Providence* (1761). Babeuf's secret movement, the discovery of which took him to the guillotine in 1797, was a communist one: the self-styled "conspiracy of the equals."[7] This list of examples could easily be extended.

Rousseau himself was sometimes emphatic enough in his condemnation of private property. For example, he wrote as follows in his *Discourse on the Origin of Inequality* (1755):

The first man who, having enclosed a piece of ground, bethought himself of saying "This is mine," and found people simple enough to believe him, was the real founder of civil society. From how many crimes, wars, and murders, from how many horrors and misfortunes might not anyone have saved mankind, by pulling up the stakes, or filling up the ditch, and crying to his fellows: "Beware of listening to this impostor; you are undone if you once forget that the fruits of the earth belong to all, and the earth itself to nobody."[8]

Nor can there be any serious doubt as to Godwin's attitude toward private property. The following passage from *Political Justice* is a sufficiently representative one. The substance of it is so excessively familiar by now, and was, indeed, so excessively familiar a hundred years ago, that it is somewhat dispiriting to remember that the passage dates from 1793:

Every man may calculate, in every glass of wine he drinks, and every ornament he annexes to his person, how many individuals have been condemned to slavery and sweat, incessant drudgery, unwholesome food, continual hardships, deplorable ignorance, and brutal insensibility, that he may be supplied with these luxuries. It is a gross imposition that men are accustomed to put upon themselves when they talk of the property bequeathed to them by their ancestors. The property is produced by the daily labour of men who are now in existence. All that their ancestors bequeathed to them was a mouldy patent which they show as a title to extort from their neighbours what the labour of those neighbours has produced.[9]

But communism was, of course, the most terrifying of all the Enlightenment theorems. Hence, even before the Revolution of 1789* had brought it home to everyone that the Enlightenment was in earnest, few people were resolute enough to remain consistent communists. Rousseau, in his *Discourse on Political Economy* (1758) – a mere three years after his *Discourse on the Origin of Inequality* – candidly contradicted what he had said in that earlier work about private property: "It is certain that the right of property is the most sacred of all the rights of citizenship. . . ."[10] Godwin, writing in 1793, was obliged to contradict himself in one and the same book. There, he simply intersperses his passages of

---

* Stove's reference is to the revolution at Versailles, which is generally dated from May 5 to October 15, 1789. Important moments included the fall of the Bastille on July 14, the formal abolition of feudalism on August 4, and the August drafting of the Declaration of the Rights of Man and of the Citizen. – Ed.

communist rhetoric (of which an example has just been given) with opposite rhetoric about the "sacredness" of property.[11]

By the 1820s, the retreat of the Enlightened from communism was almost universal. The Saint-Simonians,* for example, qualified the equality axiom itself, and sanctioned inequality of wealth where, though only where, it was based on *merit*.[12] Many others – Tom Paine, for example – decided that their real opposition was only to *inherited* inequalities of wealth, and so on.† Only a very few of the Enlightened, such as Robert Owen and Karl Marx, remained faithful to the original communist theorem. These few, however, very naturally derided the illogicality, the timidity, or (in some cases) the venality of the great majority of the Enlightened who had lost, or qualified, their earlier faith in that theorem.

---

* Claude-Henri de Rouvroy, Comte de Saint-Simon (1760–1825) is widely recognized as the founder of French socialism. His theory of class conflict between the producers (or industriels) and the parasites (or bureaucrats) predates Marx's account by half a century. – Ed.

† Thomas Paine, *The Rights of Man* (1791–1792), Part 2, ch. 5. Paine's essay was written as a response to Edmund Burke's *Reflections on the Revolution in France* (1790). – Ed.

THE MORAL VALUES of the Enlightenment, then, made benevolence the highest virtue. They enjoined, both for the sake of greatest happiness and for the sake of equality, the equalization of property; and since it was always obvious that community of property alone can ensure permanent equality of property, communism was an inevitable further consequence of these values.

But in Enlightenment's house there are many mansions. At the same time as benevolence and community of property were unfolding as obligations upon the Enlightened in general, certain quite opposite convictions on these same subjects were becoming established among a particular subgroup of the Enlightened: those, namely, whom we would nowadays call economists. One of these opposite convictions was that equality of property, if it is possible at all, could only come about through equality of *poverty*. Another was that benevolence, when it is exercised in an attempt to equalize wealth, produces — as we have seen that it certainly does in some other cases — the very opposite of the happiness it is intended to produce.

Malthus was the ablest representative of such ideas as these, but he did not originate any of them. On the contrary, every essential element of Malthus's book was in circulation well before he published his *Essay on Population* in 1798.[13] Even Mandeville's *Fable of the Bees* (1714) is in some respects a forerunner of the *Essay*, and Malthus himself refers with approval to a pamphlet by Defoe, titled *Giving Alms No Charity*, which was published in 1704. But it will be worthwhile to mention some later, and more weighty, forerunners.

Malthus believed that any human society, unless it falls into communist poverty, will always contain a majority of laborers and a minority of proprietors. More generally, he believed that there are only two possible forms which human society can take: one in which *most* people are *comparatively* poor, and one in which *everyone* is *absolutely* poor. This is the thesis that equality of property (and *a fortiori* community of property) must be equality in poverty. Now compare with this the following passage of Hume, which was published in 1751:

> But historians, and even common sense, may inform us, that, however specious these ideas of *perfect* equality may seem, they are really, at bottom, *impracticable*; and were they not so, would be extremely *pernicious* to human society. Render possessions ever so equal, men's different degrees of art, care, and industry will immediately break that equality. Or if you check these virtues, you reduce society to the most extreme indigence; and instead of preventing want and beggary in a few, render it unavoidable to the whole community.[14]

Joseph Townsend's *Dissertation on the Poor Laws* is an attack on those laws which is essentially along Malthus's lines, though published in 1785; that is, thirteen years before Malthus's book. Townsend argues that communism could only result in universal poverty, that the Poor Laws are the beginning of communism, and that they give a strong and disastrous stimulus to the increase of population. Indeed, this forgotten book is not only proto-Malthusian, but proto-Darwinian, for it contains an arresting story of what happened on the uninhabited island of Juan Fernandez when the Spaniards released first some goats there, and later some dogs.[15] (Unfortunately, I do not know how much of this story is history and how much is fiction.)

The chemist and philosopher Joseph Priestley was a dissenter in religion, a republican in politics, and an ardent sympathizer with the French Revolution. By the mid-1790s, therefore, he was an object of aversion and alarm to Malthus, Burke, and the British government. Yet in economic matters he was emphatically on the same side as Malthus; nor was this sort of combination at all uncommon at the time. Concerning the Poor Laws, Priestley wrote as follows in his *Lectures on History and General Policy* (1788):

> If every man who is reduced to poverty, by whatever means, be allowed to have a claim upon the common stock for subsistence, great numbers, who are indifferent about anything beyond a mere subsistence, will be improvident, spending everything they get in the most extravagant manner, as knowing that they have a certain resource in the provision which the law makes for them; and *the greater the provision that is made for the poor, the more poor there will be to avail themselves of*

it; as, in general, men will not submit to labour if they can live without it. By this means, man, instead of being the most provident of animals, as he naturally would be, is the most improvident of them all. Having no occasion for foresight, he thinks of nothing beyond the present moment, and thus is reduced to a condition lower than that of the beasts. *This is now become very much the case in this country, and the evil is so great and inveterate, that it is not easy to find a remedy.*[16]

Even these few references to forerunners of Malthus's *Essay* will suffice to indicate, to anyone familiar with that book, that its merits do not include great originality. But Hume, Townsend, and Priestley all had countless other intellectual preoccupations, whereas Malthus devoted his mind for several decades exclusively to this one thing: the economic consequences of the Enlightenment morality of benevolence and equality. It is the resulting comprehensiveness of treatment which gives his *Essay*, at least after the first edition, its unique merit. Malthus patiently and fairly examines every known version of the belief that economic distress can be removed by benevolence directed to the equalization or the communization of property. His conclusion is always, indeed, that benevolence so directed can in fact only *increase* economic distress. But he is never partisan, or even hasty, in coming to that conclusion.

The course of history since Malthus wrote has been such as to invest his *Essay* with ever-increasing value. At the time at which I write, 1989, his study of the economic consequences of Enlightenment ethics is even more important than it has ever been before.

As a critic of communist utopianism, Malthus indeed partly botched his work. There he attempted too much, namely, to prove it *impossible* for a communist economy to exist at all: to exist not just for thirty years, but even for one second. Yet the only thing he could point to as preventing its possibility – the fact that if communism were once established, population would press with the utmost severity upon the supply of food – was something which, according to Malthus himself, exists *already* and *always*. His argument therefore, if it had been a good one, would equally have proved the impossibility of the economic *status quo* which he was defending.*

But it is a very different matter when Malthus is attempting less: when he argues, not that communism is impossible, but that it must be, after thirty or fifty years, economically catastrophic; or when he is pointing out the disastrous effects of schemes of benevolence – such as the Poor Laws – which themselves promise far less than communist utopias do. Here, especially in editions of the *Essay* after the first, Malthus is superb.

* * *

The Poor Laws were old, dating from the reign of Elizabeth I. Yet the essence of their history can be told quickly because, as people like Malthus constantly complained, their outcome

---

* For further discussion, see D. C. Stove, "The Malthus Check" and "Population, Privilege, and Malthus' Retreat," in *On Enlightenment*, pp. 57–73, 75–91. – Ed.

could easily have been predicted in advance by anyone who possessed elementary knowledge of human nature, and who was not blinded by benevolence.

Under the Poor Laws, money was given to persons in economic distress who lived within the parish. (Hence the fact that the Poor Laws were often alternatively called "parish laws.") The money was raised by a tax falling at regular intervals on the local occupiers of land, and proportioned to the value of the land they occupied. (The occupier, of course, might or might not be the owner of the land.) The rate of taxation was set, from time to time, by local civil and ecclesiastical authorities in consultation. These authorities also appointed officers to administer the tax.

It should go without saying that the administration of the Poor Laws was always expensive, inefficient, corrupt, and vexatious, both to those who received money and to those who parted with it. Far more importantly, however, and to the immense puzzlement of almost everyone, it was found that the proportion of the population receiving money under the laws (and consequently, of course, the burden on those who paid the tax) *always increased.*

Not every year, indeed, or at a uniform rate. In fact there was a pattern of alternation between periods of "soft" and of "hard" administration of the laws. When distress among laboring men was severe, a mixture of benevolence and fear would prompt the Poor Law authorities to "soften" the laws. The amount of relief would be increased; or the conditions necessary to qualify for relief would be relaxed; or relief would be made available, not only in the supervised "workhouses" maintained for that purpose, but at the doors of the distressed persons themselves, and so on. Then, when economic conditions improved, the Poor Law authorities would be struck with horror at the cancer-like growth of the system over which they presided and would "harden" the laws once again.

Nevertheless, every fifteen years or so found the beneficiaries of the Poor Laws being a larger proportion of the population than they had been before, and the occupiers of the land, accordingly, being burdened with a higher rate of taxation than they had been before. Writers around 1800 generally estimated that about one person in seven in Britain was to some extent dependent on the Poor Laws. The rate of taxation, around the same time, had risen quickly to extraordinary levels: nearly eighteen shillings in the pound.* In 1817, two parishes in Dorsetshire were taxed at the rate of nineteen and twenty-one shillings in the pound respectively.[17] Since this was the subject of a complaint to Parliament, it was evidently exceptional; but it was not *very* exceptional. No wonder, then, that Malthus, and very many others, feared that the Poor Laws would soon ruin first the poorest tenants, then all the other tenants, and ultimately all the landowners. And how would the poor, so vastly increased by the addition of such numbers, be fed *then?*

---

* At this time, one pound equaled twenty shillings. Being taxed eighteen shillings on the pound thus meant a tax rate equal to 90 percent of the value of the land the taxpayer occupied, nineteen meant a rate equal to 95 percent, and twenty-one meant a rate equal to 105 percent. This need not involve a negative income, provided that each year the occupier of the land was able to earn an income significantly greater than the value of the land itself. For related discussion, see M. Turner and D. Mills, *Land and Property: The English Land Tax, 1692–1832* (New York: St. Martin's Press, 1986). – Ed.

MALTHUS DID NOT DENY, of course, that the Poor Laws succeeded in relieving some economic distress; but he believed that those same laws *"create* the poor which they maintain," and that they must constantly create more.[18] He had two arguments for this belief.

First, the money that some poor people receive under the Poor Laws has no tendency whatever to increase the amount of food existing. In contrast, it does have a strong tendency to increase the number of poor people, since it lightens any anxiety which its recipients may feel about how their children are to be supported. The Poor Laws tend, therefore, to increase the number of poor people without increasing the means by which they can subsist. They therefore tend to make all the poor still poorer since, as they increase in number, the price of provisions will correspondingly rise. Hence, among the poor who had previously been independent of the Poor Laws, the poorest will be driven into dependence on those laws.

Second, you cannot relieve the economic distress of certain members of a given class without deepening the distress of all the other members of it. (For example, you could not enrich just the *redheaded* poor, say, without making the economic position of all other poor people worse.) Under the Poor Laws, some of the poor are relieved, but part of the tax is raised from others: the independent poor. They are therefore made poorer, and the poorest of them must, as a result, become dependent on the Poor Laws. This effect will obviously be the more pronounced the more generous is the relief which the laws provide. (For example, better food in the workhouses, or less horrible conditions, will require a heavier burden on those who pay the tax, including the independent poor.)

It may be worthwhile to point out that the second of these arguments, unlike the first, does not depend on any assumption whatever about population; and also that Malthus, though he considered both arguments unanswerable, expressed a guarded preference for the second.[19] In any case, he gives both arguments, both in the first and in later editions of the book. He then immediately, with only trifling differences among the editions, continues as follows:

> Hard as it may appear in individual instances, dependent poverty ought to be held disgraceful. Such a stimulus seems to be absolutely necessary to promote the happiness of the great mass of mankind; and every general attempt to weaken this stimulus, however benevolent its intention, will always defeat its own purpose. If men be induced to marry from the mere prospect of parish provision, they are not only unjustly tempted to bring unhappiness and dependence upon

themselves and their children, but they are tempted, without knowing it, to injure all in the same class with themselves.

The poor-laws of England appear to have contributed to raise the price of provisions, and to lower the real price of labor. They have therefore contributed to impoverish that class of people whose only possession is their labor. It is also difficult to suppose that they have not powerfully contributed to generate that carelessness and want of frugality observable among the poor, so contrary to the disposition generally to be remarked among petty tradesmen and small farmers. The laboring poor, to use a vulgar expression, seem always to live from hand to mouth. Their present wants employ their whole attention; and they seldom think of the future. Even when they have an opportunity of saving, they seldom exercise it; but all that they earn beyond their present necessities goes, generally speaking, to the ale-house. The poor-laws may therefore be said to diminish both the power and the will to save among the common people; and thus to weaken one of the strongest incentives to sobriety and industry, and consequently to happiness.[20]

Of course the *intention* behind the Poor Laws had always been benevolent. But it is a physical impossibility, Malthus says, to lessen widespread economic distress from outside, as these laws propose to do, just as it is a physical impossibility to improve the weather by opening the barometer and pushing the needle from "Stormy" to "Settled Fair."[21]

Furthermore, the Poor Laws had *always* been an attempt to do something which is impossible:

> The famous 43rd of Elizabeth, which has been so often referred to and admired, enacts that the overseers of the poor "shall take order from time to time, by and with the consent of two or more justices, for setting to work the children of all such, whose parents shall not by the said persons be thought able to keep and maintain their children: and also such persons, married or unmarried, as, having no means to maintain them, use no ordinary and daily trade of life to get their living by; and also to raise weekly, or otherwise, by taxation of every inhabitant, and every occupier of lands in the said parish, (in such competent sums as they shall think fit), a convenient stock of flax, hemp, wool, thread, iron, and other necessary ware and stuff, to set the poor to work."
>
> What is this but saying that the funds for the maintenance of labour in this country may be increased at will, and without limit, by a *fiat* of government, or an assessment of the overseers? Strictly speaking, this clause is as arrogant and as absurd as if it had enacted that two ears of wheat should in future grow where one only had grown before. Canute, when he commanded the waves not to wet his princely foot, did not in reality assume a greater power over the laws of nature. No directions are given to the overseers how to increase the funds for the maintenance of labour; the necessity of industry, economy, and enlightened

exertion in the management of agricultural and commercial capital is not insisted on for this purpose; but it is expected that a miraculous increase of these funds should immediately follow an edict of the government used at the discretion of some ignorant parish officers.[22]

The same absurdity, Malthus points out, is at the very heart of

the common declamation on the subject of the poor, which we see so often in print, and hear continually in conversation, namely, that the market price of labour ought always to be sufficient decently to support a family, and that employment ought to be found for all those who are willing to work. [This] is in effect to say that the funds for the maintenance of labour in this country are not only infinite, but not subject to variation; and that, whether the resources of a country be rapidly progressive, slowly progressive, stationary, or declining, the power of giving full employment and good wages to the labouring classes must always remain exactly the same – a conclusion which contradicts the plainest and most obvious principles of supply and demand, and involves the absurd position that a definite quantity of territory can maintain an infinite population.[23]

The response of Marxists and other communists, when they hear Malthus's arguments, has always been to the following effect: "But these arguments, even on the very face of them, *assume* the 'laws' of supply and demand, and the subjection of labour to those 'laws.' This, however, is simply to assume the inevitability of capitalism; whereas in a communist economy, those 'laws' are abolished." But no response could be more ignorant or foolish than this.

It is simply not true that Malthus assumed the inevitability of capitalism: he did not assume the inevitability of any particular economic system. He discussed, fairly and on their own terms, the communist "systems of equality" which such people as Godwin and Owen had advocated. When Malthus is not attempting, as I said before, to prove communism utterly impossible, his objection to it, though exceedingly simple, is still devastating enough; and it by no means assumes the inevitability of capitalism.

In a communist system of equality, Malthus points out, no one need fear to worsen his own economic position, or to leave his children unprovided for, through his own improvidence or idleness. There is therefore no inducement for any man to limit the number of his children. At the same time, in a communist system, no one can hope to improve his own economic position, or his children's, by industry, sobriety, and economy. The joint result of these two circumstances must be that "the whole nation would shortly become a nation of paupers with a community of goods."[24]

Of course it is sickening to modern ears, in fact absolutely intolerable, to hear talk of "industry," "improvidence," "idleness," or the like. In 1989, not one person in fifty can hear such words without shame and indignation. We feel about them the same way as Shakespeare's Jack Cade felt, in *Henry VI, Part II*, about the filthy words that scholars use, such as "noun" and "verb."* I am sorry to give this kind of offense; but in expounding Malthus, it is quite impossible to avoid it.

In particular, Ms. Marxo-Feminist is nowadays certain to say, "Obviously, Malthus was simply taking *bourgeois* psychology for granted; but future psychology will be different." Well, she said the same thing in 1889 too, and no doubt some of her forerunners in 1789 said much the same then; and what she says may be true, at that: it is not *logically* impossible that future human psychology will be different from that of the past. But then, of course, neither is it *logically* impossible that future human bodies will grow leaves rather than hair, or that the typical result of their sexual intercourse will be a shark or a pineapple.

All that Malthus *actually* assumed were certain elements of human psychology, as past experience has disclosed them to be. Namely, he assumed an instinct of hunger in all; a sexual instinct in virtually all; a plentiful supply of laziness in the vast majority; and no shortage anywhere of selfishness, stupidity, or short-sightedness. There is, indeed, no rational way to proceed, as Malthus himself says, except on the assumption that human beings will be what past experience has uniformly shown them to *have* been.[25]

After all, those four elements of human psychology, in conjunction, are at least powerful enough to bring it about that population almost always does increase, even against colossal impediments. It increases even now, for example, in

---

* William Shakespeare, *Henry VI, Part II*, act IV, scene VII. – Ed.

the free countries, where abortion terminates millions of pregnancies every year, and contraception daily prevents many times that number.

As I have said, the surpassing merit of Malthus's *Essay*, after its first edition, is its comprehensiveness. Accordingly he does not omit to consider how, in a communist economy, population might be restrained from pressing so hard on the food supply as to ensure universal poverty. Ignoring, as he always does, the possibility of widespread contraception, he concluded – quite rightly, as far as he goes – that communists would have to resort to unprecedented *coercion*:

> It does not seem to be a necessary consequence of a system of equality that all the human passions should be at once extinguished by it; but if not, those who might wish to marry would feel it hard that they should be among the number forced to restrain their inclinations. As all would be equal, and in similar circumstances, there would be no reason whatever why one individual should think himself obliged to practise the duty of restraint more than another. The thing however must be done, with any hope of avoiding universal misery; and in a state of equality, the necessary restraint could only be effected by some general law. But how is this law to be supported, and how are the violations of it to be punished? Is the man who marries early to be pointed at with the finger of scorn? Is he to be whipped at the cart's tail? Is he to be confined for years in a prison? Is he to have his children exposed? Are not all direct punishments for an offence

of this kind shocking and unnatural to the last degree?[26]

Alas, poor innocent, ignorant, fortunate Malthus! How little, after all, even he foresaw of the realities of the politics of Enlightened persons. "Laws," forsooth, and "punishments"! As though Stalin, Mao, or Pol Pot cared any more for laws than they did for religion or bourgeois morality. They simply gave orders for millions of people to be shot or starved to death. That is, at any rate, one way in which, in communist societies, population *is* restrained. Even where, as in China at present, a woman's second or later pregnancy *must* be terminated or prevented, this is not a matter of *law*, or of punishment for the breach of a law. The Central Committee of the Communist Party, which has monopoly of the means of coercion, has simply given an order: that is all there is to it.

Neither of Malthus's arguments against the Poor Laws was ever answered. The reason is that they are unanswerable. Exemption from anxiety about how your children are to live *must* tend to produce a larger number of children than you would otherwise have had. A tax for the benefit of the poorest, falling on some of the not-quite-so-poor, *must* tend to convert some of the latter into the former.

These are propositions which are as true, and which ought to be as obvious, as the proposition that falling from an eightieth-story window *must* tend to result in injury. Of course, like that proposition, they are only assertions of tendency. The falling man *might* be saved from injury by Superman, or by a lucky whirlwind; and similarly, historical accidents might have prevented the Poor Laws from having the effect, or as much of the effect, as was reasonably to be expected from them. But, while an intervention by Superman is always possible, it remains true that falling out of eightieth-story windows is very dangerous. In the same way, while it is always possible that historical accidents should prevent a system like the Poor Laws from having its full natural effect, it remains true that such a system is very destructive of wealth, and productive of the poverty which it is intended to relieve.

Malthus, with his usual fair-mindedness, admits that the Poor Laws, having existed so long, should have had, according to his arguments, even worse effects than they actually had had. He points out several historical accidents, peculiar to Britain, which may have "cushioned" the effect of these laws. But he also points out a fact which quite certainly *did* do a great deal of cushioning and which, at the same time, was by no means accidental, but inherent in the Poor Law system itself. This was the terrific mortality among children born or raised in the workhouses. "A great part of the redundant population occasioned by the poor laws," he wrote, "is thus taken off by the operation of the laws themselves, or at least by their ill execution."[27] (But as to these last seven words, whether Malthus really believed that this effect might be accidental, or owing merely to the "ill execution" of the Poor Laws, is more than doubtful.)

* * *

The Poor Laws were only one example, though easily the most important one, of benevolence directed to the relief of poverty and the equalizing of wealth. Malthus indefatigably

examines many other schemes which had been proposed with
the same benevolent intention. Some, such as Rumford's
"cheap soup" scheme, were merely superficial.[28] Others, such
as Townsend's scheme for compulsory universal "friendly
societies," were radical indeed but, as Malthus points out,
would simply be the Poor Laws under another name and in
an aggravated form.[29] Arthur Young's proposal, for a cow
and half an acre to be given to every agricultural laborer with
three or more children, would constitute a catastrophic
encouragement to population, and so on.[30]

Thomas Paine had advocated, in *The Rights of Man*
(1791–1792), replacement of the Poor Laws by a ferocious
tax, quickly rising to twenty shillings in the pound, on all
inheritances. The proceeds were to be given to the poor in
the form of assistance to parents for the support of their children; compulsory free education; old-age pensions from the
age of fifty; workers' compensation; a gift of fifteen pounds
to *everyone* turning twenty-one; workhouses which would
admit everyone who applied for admission, subject only to
their agreeing to work under supervision; and so on.[31] The
scheme was, in short, simply the Poor Laws (as Malthus says)
"aggravated a hundred fold" and, if it were adopted, would
be sure to have the corresponding effects.[32]

In a similar vein, Malthus points out that the creation of
foundling hospitals acts, and must act, as an encouragement
to the production of illegitimate children.[33] Likewise even
private charity, if it is elicited by *mere* distress, must have
exactly the same kind of effects as public charity; it must penal-
ize its non-recipients, and thus make more of them objects for
charity, while it tends to free the minds of recipients from

uneasiness concerning their children. The only thing that makes private charity vastly preferable to public is the fact that it operates on a vastly smaller scale.[34]

* * *

It is the literal truth – no matter how unlikely it may appear to my readers – that Malthus was second to no man in England in the strength of his desire to alleviate the misery of the great majority of his fellow countrymen. Nor did he entirely despair of progress towards that end. He saw some hope in the then recently instituted savings banks,[35] and much more hope in making elementary education, especially economic education, available to the poor;[36] but he also told his countrymen unpalatable truths. He told them that governments, or the rich, *cannot*, as a mere matter of fact, increase the supply of food, or decrease (except by murder or the like) the ever-increasing number of claimants for food; that the attempt to equalize wealth, if it succeeded, would replace the comparative poverty of most by the absolute poverty of all; that a poor man's only chance of improving his condition lies, not in any external circumstances, but in his own industry, sobriety, and economy.

These are truths which are so extremely remote from general consciousness now, while utilitarianism is almost universal, that it may be advisable to mention that Malthus believed them *in conjunction with* utilitarianism. He *shared* with the Enlightened in general, and with his utopian adversaries in particular, the belief that the greatest happiness of the greatest number is the test of morality. He shared their belief that benevolence is the highest virtue. He merely pointed out that benevolence, if directed to relieving poverty and equalizing wealth, is, as a matter of fact, productive of misery rather than happiness.

But there was also in Malthus a deeper and better moral vein at odds with his utilitarianism. He was no Burke, indeed, or even a de Tocqueville. Still, he dimly discerned, in the overwhelming drive for universal happiness which was engulfing Europe, the presage of a new and terrible world: a world in which, through the hopeless attempt to abolish poverty and inequality, there might *really* be abolished all science and art, all religion and morality, and the disinterestedness of the student, the soldier, and the saint alike:

> To the laws of property and marriage, and to the apparently narrow principle of self-interest which prompts each individual to exert himself in bettering his condition, we are indebted for all the noblest exertions of human genius, for everything that distinguishes the civilised from the savage state.[37]

WHAT A MESSAGE from a vanished world is that quotation! Malthus was the last thinker of major importance who was an unqualified supporter of private property, the bourgeois family, and "the apparently narrow principle of self-interest." Indeed, for a hundred years he was the last thinker of any importance at all to be an unswerving defender of these three things. His *Essay* opened the fateful nineteenth-century contest between capitalism on the one hand and, on the other, the benevolent determination to relieve poverty and equalize wealth. That determination included, of course, a determination to acknowledge the economic and social "rights of women," both within and without marriage, as being equal to those of men.

This contest was not one between Enlightenment and something else. It was a contest within the Enlightenment, between Enlightened *economics* and Enlightened *ethics*. But it was not, on that account, a contest any the less fateful for the entire civilized world. Nor, for all its fatefulness, did it even last long. The outcome could be read off the face of Britain as early as 1860.* Malthus lost. Benevolence won, as Australians say, "with daylight second."

For a few decades it might have seemed as though Malthus

---

* The date is meant as an approximation. For example, Karl Marx's *Critique of Political Economy* and John Stuart Mill's *Essay on Liberty* both appeared in 1859. Mill's *Utilitarianism* followed shortly afterwards, in 1863. – Ed.

might win. British governments, almost from the time the *Essay* was first published, recognized the value of his economic advice. The Benthamites embraced his economics enthusiastically, except for his attitude towards contraception, which they thought merely quaint. Through their influence, the Poor Laws were reformed in 1834 along the lines of which Malthus (who died that year) would have approved. But after the mid-century, the triumph of benevolence and equality was never in doubt.* In theory, of course, the Liberal Party was the champion of capitalism, but in fact it became, as every political party then had to become, simply one of the contenders in the benevolence competition.

Long after the outcome of the contest was clear, vestiges of the Malthusian side remained unextinguished. As long as books by Samuel Smiles, with titles like *Self-Help* (1859), *Thrift* (1875), and *Duty* (1880), sold many thousands of copies – as they did up to about 1900 – there was still some resistance to the party of benevolence and equality. But by 1900, after all, the Jazz Age was only twenty years away. When it arrived, Samuel Smiles would be numbered among the countless relics, part comic and part horrific, of the Victorian age, and the very names of his books, and their author, would seem to Enlightened persons a joke almost too good to be true.

Long after Malthus's death, there was an isolated and anomalous outcrop of his influence in America. This was the "Social Darwinism" of the late nineteenth and early twentieth centuries. The name of Darwin was brought into it, of course,

* One final, representative attempt at this time to stop the tide was Charles Gourard's *Socialism Unmasked* (London: George Slater, 1850). – Ed.

mainly because most people did not know that he had got from Malthus the idea that population always presses upon the supply of food. The anomalous thing about Social Darwinism was that it was not (as it was later represented by the benevolent party to have been) peculiar to certain "ruthless capitalists." It was also adopted by many American socialists of the time. W. T. Mills, author of *The Struggle for Existence* (7th ed., 1904), was among the examples of this curious eddy in the contest between capitalism and benevolence. Similarly, though even more oddly, some Russian revolutionary groups of the 1880s based their claims to leadership on their having been *"naturally selected"* under Czarist pressure!

But the real fact of the matter is that Malthus had lost the contest almost before he began to fight it: so overwhelming, even then, was the torrent of Enlightened benevolence. In a note which he appended to his *Essay* in 1803, he wrote as follows:

> During the late dearths, half of the gentlemen and clergymen of the kingdom richly deserved to have been prosecuted for sedition. After inflaming the minds of the common people against the farmers and corn-dealers, by the manner in which they talked of them or preached about them, it was but a feeble antidote to the poison which they had infused, coldly to observe that, however the poor might be oppressed or cheated, it was their duty to keep the peace.[38]

Malthus was no doubt right in saying that half the gentlemen and clergy had recently merited prosecution for sedition, but when the seditious reach that number, it is idle to talk of prosecuting them. The probability then is, rather, that it will soon be the chance of the seditious to prosecute any opposition to *them* as being seditious.

* * *

Community of property as a cure for poverty and inequality is not an idea which waited until the late nineteenth century to become formidable. On the contrary, from 1789 on, communist ideas sprang up everywhere, with irrepressible exuberance; and not only ideas, either: communist realities sprang up in many places in England, France, Germany, and America. But their favored place, partly because land was comparatively cheap there, was America.

From New England to Oregon, communist communities came into existence all through the nineteenth century and beyond. There were communities of Owenite communists, Fourierite communists, Icarians, Rappists, Shakers, Perfectionists. . . . The list goes on and on, and the numbers of people involved were not contemptible. The Shakers, at the height of their fortunes, could boast of scores of settlements scattered across many states, each one containing a hundred to two hundred people. There are two valuable contemporary surveys of this great, though now forgotten, explosion of communist realities: one by C. A. Nordhoff,[39] a sympathetic outsider, and one from the inside by J. H. Noyes,[40] who was the leader of the Perfectionists.

Of course none of these communities did what they all began by expecting to do: convert the world, beginning with their unregenerate neighbors, by the manifest superiority of communist life. Most of the communities were very short-lived. But even as late as 1969, at Oneida in New York State, industrial relations in certain factories still showed some faint traces of the Perfectionists' communism;[41] and the Shakers are not quite extinct, I believe, even now. These two groups undoubtedly owed a good deal of their success to their having learned something from Malthus. The Perfectionists practiced contraception, eugenics, and the marriage of all the women to all the men. The Shakers practiced complete sexual abstinence. (They also made, though without saying a word, the most telling criticism that has ever been made of the bourgeois family: their longevity was extraordinary.)

But the success or failure of these practical trials of communism is not historically important. What is important is the fact that they were made at all in the numbers they were. The fact, in other words, that from Britain, France, Germany, and America itself there came an endless stream of men and women not merely willing but determined to surrender their lives and their property to a communist society: to "Harmony" (as both Owenites and Fourierites sometimes said), or to "Association" (as the Fourierites also said), or to "Cooperation," or to "Community."

Nor did this crusade – for such it really was – enlist only the ignorant poor. The general level of cultivation in the communist societies was certainly low, and showed no tendency to rise. Many Shakers, for example, began and remained illiterate. But at Brook Farm and Fruitlands, on the other hand, the Fourierite-communist experiments were participated in by some of the most privileged and cultivated of New England spirits: a Nathaniel Hawthorne, an Elizabeth Peabody, a George Ripley. And after all, Coleridge and Southey had set out in 1794, when they were both still Enlightened, to set up a communist paradise on the banks of the Susquehanna. (In fact they got no further than Bristol, where both got married instead; but that does not affect the point.) Thomas Hughes, MP, author of *Tom Brown's School Days* (1857), founded a "model society" in Tennessee in the 1880s, naming it "Rugby" in memory of his revered headmaster, Dr. Thomas Arnold. You cannot get much more respectable than that.

For every person who actually joined a communist society in the nineteenth century, it is reasonable to suppose that there were at least twenty others who were strongly drawn to the idea, but who were never quite resolute enough to put it into practice. This forgotten phase of communist (and American) history is, therefore, extremely revealing. It suddenly shows us, as in a lightning flash, how widespread and intense was the rejection of Malthus's ideals. For the ruling object of these many thousands of lives was precisely to *escape from* private property, self-reliance, and "the laws of marriage."

* * *

The hopelessness of Malthus's cause can also be illustrated in another, perhaps even more striking, way.

I pointed out (in section IV above) the falsity of the widespread belief that the Enlightenment was friendly to the institution of private property. On the contrary, I said, communism follows easily, and indeed follows twice over, from the axioms of the Enlightenment.

Of course, logic is not life. Even if Enlightened people *logically* should have been enemies of capitalism, it does not follow that in fact they all were, or even that any of them were. Indeed, there was (as I said in section IV) a widespread retreat by the Enlightened from their own communist theorem after the shock of 1789.

But now let us ask: *how far* did they ever retreat from it? How many people were there in the nineteenth century who, while remaining Enlightened on the fundamental subject of religion, shared Malthus's views on property and marriage? How many critics of Christianity were there who were not also critics of capitalism?

As far as Britain is concerned, I venture to affirm that the answer to this question is just three, with at most three other "debatables." The three are Herbert Spencer, Leslie Stephen, and Samuel Butler; the debatables are Harriet Martineau, H. T. Buckle, and T. H. Huxley; and this is, of course, three-to-six out of many hundreds of atheists, agnostics, secularists, Unitarians, etc., etc.

Two classic books are essential reading in this connection: A. W. Benn's *History of English Rationalism in the Nineteenth Century* (1906),[42] and J. M. Robertson's *History of Free-Thought in the Nineteenth Century* (1929).[43] The former book relates almost exclusively to Britain, while the latter covers all Europe and beyond. Between them, these books constitute exhaustive biographical dictionaries of the critics of religion between 1800 and 1900. You will search their total of two thousand pages almost in vain for individuals who shared Malthus's views on the relief of poverty and the equalization of wealth.

People of the Joseph Priestley type, who combined Enlightened religion and politics with Malthusian economics, had been common enough in the late eighteenth century; but they could breathe only with difficulty the benevolence-saturated air of the nineteenth century. Even their nearest descendants, the Benthamites, found it necessary, after about 1825, to grow what later came to be called "a social conscience." It did not come easily to them, but they did it. In fact the most widely admired social conscience of the whole century was the one finally grown by the Crown Prince of Benthamism, John Stuart Mill: a clear case of the kind that Samuel Smiles loved, of the triumph of effort over adverse initial circumstances.

Of the hundreds of enemies of Christianity who are surveyed in the books by Benn and Robertson, perhaps not one in ten was ever a communist. Yet virtually every one of them hungered for the relief of poverty and the equalization of wealth, as prescribed by the Enlightenment axioms they shared with the communists. They all agonized, to a greater or lesser degree, over what they began, in the 1830s, to call "the social problem."

Indeed, the universality of this new phrase among Enlightened people during most of the nineteenth century is almost sufficient proof in itself of the utter eclipse of Malthus's point of view. For what the phrase designated – the fact that most people were comparatively poor and a few comparatively rich – had, of course, *always* existed; and, according to Malthus, always would exist, unless replaced by the absolute poverty of all. It had simply never been accounted a *problem* until Enlightened benevolence came along.

What's Wrong with Benevolence

The equalization of wealth had always been acknowledged to necessitate, as I said earlier, a revolution in the status of women. That, in turn, meant revolution for the institution of the bourgeois family. So let us look again through the books by Robertson and Benn and ask: how many of these religiously Enlightened persons were, as Malthus was, an unqualified defender of the bourgeois family? The answer to this question is the same as to the earlier one: almost none. If anything, the family excited even greater detestation among the Enlightened, from Shelley at the start of the century to Ibsen at its end, than private property did.

So utterly false, then, is the widespread belief that capitalism and religious Enlightenment are natural allies; still more false is the belief that the latter is a secret servant of the former. Quite the contrary: Robert Owen and Karl Marx spoke the truth when they said that only illogicality or timidity prevented most Enlightened people from being communists. But, as we have just seen, even in real life they *fell only a little short* of being so. The Enlightenment, then, remained substantially faithful to those of its axioms which had all along prescribed communism.

* * *

The irrepressible proliferation in the nineteenth century of communist and near-communist enterprises proves conclusively that there was an almost-universal reaction against private property, the bourgeois family, and self-reliance. The religiously Enlightened, as we have just seen, were united in their opposition to these three Malthusian ideals, and by about 1870 they had enjoyed, with the help of Darwinism, a complete intellectual victory over religion.* It was at this time, too, in 1867, that the franchise in Britain was enormously extended.

With these circumstances, Britain's economic course was irrevocably fixed for the next hundred years. It would be overwhelmingly directed towards relieving poverty and equalizing wealth.

Malthus had proposed that the relief provided by the Poor Laws should be reduced almost to nothing, by gradual stages well publicized in advance, and that it should then be replaced by nothing except private charity. In fact, the Poor Laws lost their importance in the 1870s, but only because they were merging by then into a system of the same kind, only on a scale many times larger: the welfare state. This economic system first began to take shape in the last quarter of the nineteenth century, and gathered increasing momentum for the next hundred years. Its growth was spectacularly accelerated after each of the two world wars.

The characteristic features of this benevolent system are far too familiar to need detailed description. They include unemployment "relief"; old-age pensions for all; state-subsidized education, medicine, and housing; state-prescribed minimum wages; state-prescribed hours and conditions of work; work-

---

* The date is again meant to be approximate. For example, Charles Darwin's *On the Origin of Species by Natural Selection* appeared in 1859, *The Variation of Animals and Plants under Domestication* in 1868, and *The Descent of Man* in 1871. In addition, T. H. Huxley's *Theory of Biogenesis* and A. R. Wallace's *Contributions to the Theory of Natural Selection* both appeared in 1870. – Ed.

ers' compensation; pensions for unmarried mothers; etc., etc. All these things, as well as the cost of administering them, are of course paid for out of the proceeds of taxes, levied principally on annual income, but also on inheritances and indeed on everything which might conceivably give any citizen whatever the smallest economic advantage over the poorest of his fellows.

In short, the scheme proposed by the revolutionary Thomas Paine that wealth should be equalized by redistributive taxation is now, and has been for a hundred years, the actual economic practice of Britain, as it is (with some differences of degree) in all advanced free countries. Yet Malthus had considered Paine's scheme too self-evidently fatal to human happiness to deserve detailed criticism.

So staggeringly complete, then, was the victory of Enlightened benevolence over capitalism; or so completely, in other words, did the determination to relieve poverty and equalize wealth triumph over "the laws of property and marriage" and "the apparently narrow principle of self-interest."

VIII

And yet, of course, Malthus was proved right after all. For while the vast majority of Enlightened and benevolent people were still wringing their hands over "the social problem," a handful of them actually *did* what Enlightened benevolence had always enjoined them to do: in 1917* they abolished private property and the family, and propelled the Russian Empire into disaster, as inevitably as if a canoe and its passengers had been propelled over Niagara Falls.

How greatly human happiness was increased as a result, it cannot be necessary by now to inquire. Poverty fell upon Russia like an armed man upon a defenseless enemy, exactly as Malthus had said it would; and not only as he said it would,

---

* The Bolshevik Revolution of October 1917 was preceded by a February Revolution of liberal intelligentsia, which secured the abdication of Czar Nicholas II at Pskov on March 15. A first, abortive attempt by the Bolsheviks to seize power then occurred in July. Four months later, Lenin led a more successful second revolt against Kerensky's government in the Winter Palace on November 6 and 7. The term "October Revolution" comes from the Julian calendar, which in 1917 was thirteen days behind the Western calendar. After moving the capital from Petrograd to Moscow on March 10, 1918, a new Soviet Constitution was brought into effect in July; this was despite the fact that civil war was to continue within what would become the new Soviet empire for nearly three years. — Ed.

but from the homely cause which he had said would produce it: the fact that where no one can hope to improve his own or his children's economic position, or fear to worsen it, no one will work or save.

Again exactly as Malthus had predicted, coercion was introduced on a scale without precedent in human history. It had to be. For, in the absence of that "cash-nexus"* which Marx and Lenin hated so much, there is only one corrective to idleness and improvidence: the terror-nexus.

Over a large part of Europe, the Enlightenment had already broken the priestly and political fetters that seemingly had been placed so arbitrarily on the human spirit. Only the economic fetters remained and, in Russia in 1917, these too were broken at long last. Shelley's Prometheus finally was unbound – and turned out to be Joseph Stalin unbound.

But it is ridiculous to attribute any important part of what followed to the personal defects of Stalin. His personal defects were not unique, or even exceptional. The only unique thing about Stalin was that he was the first man able, as well as willing, to compel obedience to the longstanding injunctions of Enlightened benevolence: to get rid of private property and the family. Given a monopoly of power, as he was, any consistent disciple of the Enlightenment would have done essentially the same things as Stalin.

---

* The term itself originated in Thomas Carlyle's 1839 essay "Chartism"; it received its more widespread usage after appearing in Karl Marx and Frederick Engels' *Communist Manifesto* in 1848: "The bourgeoisie, wherever it has got the upper hand, has put an end to all feudal, patriarchal, idyllic relations. It has pitilessly torn asunder the motley feudal ties that bound man to his 'natural superiors,' and has left no other nexus between people than naked self-interest, than callous 'cash payment.'" (sec. I) – Ed.

What's Wrong with Benevolence

*　*　*

Looking back at the Bolshevik Revolution, we can see now that the Enlightened for two hundred years before – all the critics of religion in the eighteenth century, all the republicans, all the secularists of the nineteenth century in agony over "the social problem," all the "emancipators" of women – resemble nothing so much as a group of innocent and foolish children, playing with their canoes in some quiet shallows, a mile upstream from Niagara. In the shallows they had proved themselves to be so strong, and no one had come to serious harm: why should they not try the deeper water?

The result vindicated not only Malthus, but all those who had tried, from whatever motives, to restrain these foolish children. All the conservatives, including of course the grasping factory owners, the brutal landlords, the time-serving clergy, and the unjust magistrates, had warned them that their activities, if continued, would result in some catastrophe without precedent in history. But these warnings, coming as they did from such un-Enlightened and plainly self-interested sources, in fact only served to *deepen* the children's belief in their own moral and intellectual superiority. The one thing which never occurred to them was that these warnings might be simply and literally true.

But they were. J. S. Mill had called the Conservatives "the stupidest party,"* and on the whole he was right. Add to that,

* J. S. Mill, "Considerations on Representative Government," in *Essays on Politics and Society*, Collected Works of John Stuart Mill, vol. 19, ed. J. M. Robson (Toronto and Buffalo: University of Toronto Press, 1977), p. 452, footnote. – Ed.

its members were unfeeling. But they were also right; and though it may be different in philosophy or mathematics or physics, in practical life being right is more important than anything else; certainly more important than being Enlightened, or benevolent, or both.

* * *

Was there anyone who *predicted* the Bolshevik Revolution, or anything like it? *Could* anyone have predicted it? Predicted it rationally, I mean, as an outcome to be expected from the stupendous backwater of Enlightened benevolence which had been increasing for two hundred years?

Of course the *Enlightened* could not predict it. The children just went on playing happily with their various canoes: anti-censorship, abolition of the House of Lords, the injustice suffered by Oscar Wilde, or whatever it might be. After 1905, J. M. Robertson felt some slight uneasiness about some of his socialist allies, especially foreign ones. Still, that was as far as it went, even with him; and Robertson would have stood out in any company for his learning, intelligence, and moral character, while among the Enlightened he was a man in a million.

But hardly anyone else seems to have been very much more prescient than the Enlightened themselves. Of course many people, especially Roman Catholics such as W. H. Mallock, could see, and did say, that some unprecedented catastrophe lay ahead *if* certain Enlightened tendencies continued to gain ground; but such conditional propositions are not at all the same thing as actual predictions.

W. R. Greg, in *Rocks Ahead, or the Warnings of Cassandra*

(1874), and Robert Flint, in *Socialism* (1894), came the closest I know of to a prediction of Niagara. Both men were theists; both understood the significance of the extension of the franchise in Britain, and of the defeat of religion by Darwinism. Flint's predictions are more accurate than Greg's, but then, of course, he had the advantage of having watched an extra twenty years of the progress of socialism at home and abroad. But even Flint's book is chiefly an illustration of the utter unimaginability, in advance, of what the politics of Enlightened benevolence would really be like. Flint could foresee nothing worse than civil war followed by a military dictatorship. The idea that a communist country would be what it turned out to be – a gigantic cemetery-prison – did not even cross his mind.

I do not believe that anyone could rationally have predicted the Bolshevik Revolution, but not because Enlightened benevolence had not given plenty of warnings of its enormous capacity to cause misery. It had: in France in 1789, 1848, and 1871,* and in Britain, by way of the Poor Laws first, and then by way of the welfare state. But even the most powerful intelligence could never have anticipated, from *that* body of evidence, the effects which were to flow from the decision of the German generals to give Lenin the chance, and the money, to dismantle Russia.

---

* All three years are significant. The French Revolution occurred in 1789. In 1848, the same year Karl Marx and Frederick Engels released their *Communist Manifesto*, the February Revolution resulted in the abdication of King Louis-Philippe, bringing to an end the 1814 restoration. Finally, in 1871 the Paris Commune briefly came to power. – Ed.

ADMITTING THAT twentieth-century communism could not have been predicted, has anything been *learned* from it? Now that it has existed for seventy-two years, has anything been learned about the effects of benevolence when it is directed to relieving poverty and equalizing wealth? More specifically, has anything about this been learned by Enlightened people in free countries?

Little or nothing. Even now, when there is no longer any dispute about the *facts* of communist life, these facts seem, somehow, to count for nothing with most Enlightened people. Every new communist movement or government in Central America or Africa is as sure of a welcome from most Enlightened people today as it was from their grandparents, if Enlightened, in 1910.

This ineducability of the Enlightened about communism is evidently constitutional, and it is certainly depressing. But it should not be found mysterious, as it often is. The explanation of it is obvious.

All of us Enlightened (or so near to all as to make no difference) still share the Enlightenment's estimate of benevolence as the highest virtue. We are all enthusiasts for the relief of poverty and the equalization of wealth. We are all still, on balance, enemies of the bourgeois family. In addition, we all know that the communists, at bottom, are impelled by benevolence, and are even firmer friends to equality of wealth than we are, and firmer enemies of the bourgeois family. How, then, could communism not be an object of indestructible goodwill among us Enlightened?[44]

WILL ENLIGHTENED people *ever* learn that benevolence, if directed to relieving poverty and equalizing wealth, always tends to make poverty more widespread?

This question would be a momentous one for future human happiness in any case, but two recent events have invested it with an additional interest. One is the surprising revival, in free countries in the last twenty years, of enthusiasm for "the free market," as we now say. The other is the even more surprising admission, by Russian and Chinese leaders in the last five years, that, as Malthus had said in 1798, communism entails poverty.

These events are so recent, and so surprising, that it is hard for us to see them in their right proportions. We cannot be sure, in either case, whether they represent the shape of things to come, or only a momentary "wobble" in the careers of the welfare state and of communism, respectively. Will our recent enthusiasm for the free market result in the welfare state being dismantled? Will the communists' recent disgust with communism result in a lasting alleviation of their poverty and terror?

At the present moment, all around the world, there are

very many people who, though scarcely daring to believe the encouraging signs before their eyes, incline to answer yes to both of these questions.[45] They may be right, and it is to be hoped, for the sake of human happiness, that they are; but I think that they are wrong both times. I do not believe that the welfare state will be dismantled, and still less that communism will be. Indeed, I think that both communism and the welfare state will continue to grow. I therefore think it more probable that some or all of the welfare states will go over Niagara than that any of the communist states will succeed in climbing back up it.

* * *

It is true that there has been a vast amount of enthusiastic talk in the free countries for several decades about dismantling the welfare state, or at least about greatly reducing its size. Indeed, all the major political parties are by now agreed (at least at election time) on the urgent necessity of doing this; but nothing of the kind ever happens, whichever party is elected. All the talk goes for nothing. Indeed it goes for less than nothing: the welfare state still grows proportionately larger every year, as it has done for a hundred years. It is the story of the Poor Laws all over again; and just as in that case, most people are puzzled as to why it should be so.

Yet a sufficient explanation of the inaction of our governments is obvious even on the very surface of things. These governments are elected by universal adult franchise; but an electorally decisive proportion of the voters – in some countries, approaching a quarter – either is employed by government or is dependent to a significant extent on some welfare program. In these circumstances it is merely childish to expect the welfare state to be reduced, at least while there is universal suffrage. A government that did away with free education, for example, or socialized medicine simply could not be re-elected. Indeed, it would be lucky to see out its term of office.

* * *

Malthus had proposed a *"very gradual"* abolition of the Poor Laws.[46] But in doing so he was, unfortunately, forgetting his own fundamental insight: that a system like the Poor Laws, or the welfare state, is what we now call a "positive feedback system." It constantly *creates more* of the poverty which it exists to relieve. A very gradual abolition of the welfare state, therefore, would have to contend against the mournful fact that the more gradual it was, the more welfare state there would be to abolish. This obstacle is quite independent of the *electoral* one: it would remain, whether there were a universal franchise, a restricted franchise, or no elections at all.

We have seen that Malthus's basic argument, slightly generalized, was the following: any attempt to relieve widespread poverty from outside rewards the recipient of the relief and thus brings more people into the relief system. It also penalizes the non-recipients and thus forces some of the poorest of them into the relief system. Hence, every attempt to relieve widespread poverty from outside actually tends to make the poverty more widespread.

I repeat – but it cannot be emphasized too much – that this argument does not depend on any assumption in favor of capitalism. All it depends on are certain assumptions of a commonsense kind about human psychology. It makes no difference whatever to Malthus's argument where the wealth which is supposed to be going to relieve poverty comes from. It must, of course, come from someone or something that *has* it; but this someone or something might be the rich, or the community, or the "surplus value" of labor, or benevolent Martians, or whatever. Wherever the wealth comes from, it will still have the two effects which Malthus said it would: rewarding the recipients and penalizing the poorest of the non-recipients, and in both of these ways increasing the number of those who qualify for relief. We ought therefore to try to reconcile ourselves to Malthus's general conclusion: that it is impossible to relieve widespread poverty from outside.

Malthus himself implies that there are certain exceptions to this conclusion, though he thinks that they are economically unimportant ones. The kind of example he gives, however, is not only not an exception but, in fact, a resounding confirmation of the rule. Malthus reminds us that many working men fall into poverty from causes quite unconnected with habits of idleness and improvidence, but simply (for example) from breaking a leg or an arm. In such cases as these, he says, even "by affording the most indiscriminate assistance . . . we are in little danger of encouraging people to break arms and legs."[47]

Sancta simplicitas! Malthus, we learn, could no more foresee the realities of the welfare state than he could the realities of communism. He would thus find the operations of our present workers' compensation laws very instructive. For one of the purposes of these laws, as every citizen of a welfare state knows, is to regulate a traffic, which has existed for nearly a hundred years, in self-inflicted injuries. Even if Malthus cannot be blamed for not foreseeing these things, it was against his own economics, and indeed against common sense, to suppose that guaranteed compensation for broken legs would not make people more careless and, therefore, more likely to break a leg.

People were puzzled in Malthus's time why the Poor Laws never effectively relieved poverty but, on the contrary, always found more poverty needing to be relieved. People are similarly puzzled now why the welfare state never achieves its objects but, instead, always finds that a greater proportion of people is entitled to its assistance. But Malthus solved this mystery by pointing out that such systems *must* tend to create more of the very poverty which they are meant to relieve.

It does not follow, of course, that this tendency will always be realized in fact, or that the welfare state *cannot* now be reversed, or at least prevented from growing. But it does follow that it will continue to grow unless it is prevented from doing so by some counteracting cause. Any such counteracting cause will have to be new: there has been nothing in the last hundred years which has been able to prevent the welfare state from increasing. It will also have to be *powerful*: more powerful, at any rate, than the resolutions of democratic governments which have been resolving for twenty years to "cut back on welfare," with no visible result whatsoever. All right: look around at our present society and ask yourself what new and powerful force is at work which might be equal to the task of stopping the growth of the welfare state. Who or what will bell the cat?

The chidings of economists certainly will not do it, and still less the chidings of essayists. What *is* to do it, then? Only one answer ever seems to be so much as suggested. This is the immense burden of taxation which is required to pay for welfare programs.

But this hope is groundless. The taxpayers groan, indeed, but something like a fifth of them are also *dependent upon* government by way of employment or some type of welfare program. They might be better off in the long run if the welfare state were reduced; but at least in the short run they simply would be out of a job, or at least poorer than they are at present, and how many citizens of the welfare state are in a position to cope with even *middle*-term economic setbacks?

But it is not narrowly economic considerations which are really decisive here. How would we taxpayers respond to an offer by government to halve our present taxes in return for the abolition of free education and socialized medicine? In other words, which would we citizens of the welfare state rather do: continue paying our present level of taxation, or bear all the cost of, and responsibility for, our own and our children's health care and education?

To anyone who knows us, the answer to this question cannot possibly be in doubt. The second alternative would, of course, cost us less money than the first alternative does, but the burden of responsibility which the second entails, the demands which it would make on us for energy and self-reliance, simply puts it out of our psychological reach.

This brings us to the root of the evil, and to the root cause which will prevent the welfare state from being dismantled: us. The kind of *character*, in other words, which has been formed by centuries of Enlightened benevolence, and especially by the last hundred years of the welfare state.

Malthus wrote his *Essay* in order to combat the belief, which was widespread and rapidly gaining ground in his time, that inequality of wealth is an *accident*: that if most people are comparatively poor and a few comparatively rich, this can only be due to the selfishness of the rich, or to the wickedness or incompetence of governments. Malthus tried to dispel this belief by exposing the fallaciousness of the inference from "There are very many poor people" to "We can and should relieve their poverty."

He did expose its fallaciousness, too, by proving that any attempt to relieve widespread poverty from outside in fact will tend to spread the poverty wider, only no one took any notice after a little while (as we saw in section VII). Malthus's proof was no sort of match for the strength of Enlightened benevolence. The determination to relieve poverty and equalize wealth went on gathering strength throughout the nineteenth century.

What is important for *our* future is the fact that the benevolence juggernaut has *continued* to gain strength up to the present hour, and that it *still* gains strength. To try to bring this fact home to the reader, I adduce the (true) Dickensian tale of the prisoners' Christmas pudding, and its partial continuation in George Orwell.

In the English city of Gloucester in 1842, a poor man deliberately committed a certain trifling offense against the law in order to get himself put in the local prison for a few days. The reason was that it was just before Christmas and he knew that, on that one day each year, prisoners were given treacle-suet pudding with raisins. But word of the man's stratagem happened to reach the prison authorities and they cancelled Christmas pudding for all the prisoners, and for good.

This story is told in *Sixty Years of an Agitator's Life* (1892), the autobiography of G. J. Holyoake.[48] Holyoake was a paradigm Enlightened figure of his time: indefatigably anti-religious, democratic, a friend and historian of "cooperation," fundraiser for Garibaldi, etc., etc. He tells the story, of course, with many expressions of compassion for the prisoner, and of scorn and contempt for the prison authorities. Holyoake was himself in the same prison at the time, on account of some of his anti-religious utterances.

Now, how many people, at the time of the event itself, in 1842, would have considered that the prison authorities had acted rightly? Probably only a minority even then, but by no means a tiny minority. When Holyoake told the story fifty years later, how many people would then have been on the authorities' side of the matter? It is safe to say, hardly one in a hundred. And what about *now?* I am confident that the reader will agree with me that not one person in a thousand now would consider the authorities to have acted rightly.

They had, though. (There goes the sympathy of every one of my readers!) The authorities found that they had unknowingly offered an incentive which was sufficient to make one man prefer being a prisoner to being a non-prisoner. And which was more likely, that he was the only man in Gloucester susceptible to this incentive, or that he was one of many? Prisoners are supported entirely at the expense of non-prisoners; additional prisoners must, therefore, make

non-prisoners poorer; and better conditions in prison cannot
fail to make prison more attractive. (If you *still* believe that
the authorities should not have cancelled the Christmas pudding, ask yourself why you do *not* believe that they should
have added cream to the pudding, or given every prisoner a
present of cash at Christmas as well.) Thus has our benevolence pressure been constantly rising, since 1842 at least.

Let us make a test closer to our own time. George Orwell
was not one of the poor, but in *Down and Out in Paris and
London* (1933) he recorded his experiences during a time
when he was pretending to be poor. Orwell never mentions,
though he almost certainly knew, that this charade was a re-
enactment of an earlier one by another socialist, Jack London, as described in his book *People of the Abyss* (1903).
Orwell's book has been very widely read, and deservedly
admired. One of the most vivid parts of it concerns the
tramps who then walked English roads in considerable numbers. Their misery was extreme: always underfed or badly
fed, without shelter by day, and enduring at night the intense
discomforts and humiliations of a workhouse – when they
were lucky enough to gain admission to one.

Now, it is perfectly certain that Orwell intended his readers to conclude that the lives of these people ought to be
made less miserable. It is equally certain that virtually every
one of his readers *did* draw that conclusion. Indeed, the possibility of *not* drawing it never crossed their minds, any more
than it had crossed Orwell's. Yet *from what* were the readers
supposed to conclude this? Why, just from the obvious fact
that there were all these very poor people. . . .

But this, of course, is simply the old and fatal inference

which Malthus had exposed long before. Tramps are supported entirely at the expense of non-tramps; hence you cannot improve the economic condition of tramps without depressing some non-tramps into tramphood. Nor can you do so without rewarding existing tramps, and thus encouraging some other people to be tramps. Yet how many of Orwell's readers, from that day to this, ever thought, however dimly, thoughts like *these?* It is safe to say, not one in a hundred thousand.

Orwell, being a socialist, probably thought that the misery of the tramps had some special connection with capitalism, but it had not. Under any economic system whatever, and wherever the money supposed to relieve tramp misery comes from, it must at least come from non-tramps, and therefore depress *their* condition, while also making tramphood more attractive than it was before.

This craze for economic benevolence – the belief that it is possible to relieve widespread poverty from outside – deserves to be called *the* economic illusion of the Enlightenment epoch, which began around 1700. What I have tried to bring home to the reader, by referring to Holyoake and Orwell, is the fact that this craze has continued to the present hour, and is now even stronger than ever. So far are we from having learned, from the communist example, what economic effects to expect from benevolence that we are even *more* in love with benevolence now than we were before 1917.

Nowadays, the inference from "There are very many of these poor people, the Xs" to "We can and should relieve the poverty of the Xs" is advanced for every value of X whatever: the unemployed, the illegitimate, the unmarried mothers, the Ethiopians.... Nor does this benevolent inference ever meet with the slightest demur. How could it? Hardly a single person now alive has ever so much as *heard* that the inference *might* be resisted. Fewer still have ever learned that it can be, has been, and should be *rationally* resisted.*

Accordingly, journalists now find it exceptionally easy to prove both the righteousness of their hearts and the clearness of their vision. All they need do is go to Buenos Aires, Bombay, Johannesburg, or wherever, and report in an article that great inequality of wealth exists there: "Shanties half a mile from palaces," etc., etc. This report is true, and the inference from it to the conclusion that *it need not, and should not, be so* is no inference at all to those who report it: to them, the fact seems to speak for itself. They share with communism the indestructible Enlightenment sympathy for benevolence as a cure for poverty and inequality. So there will also be a suggestion in the journalist's article that, when the local communists take over and obliterate the present shocking inequality of wealth, it will be no more than a just retribution – "whatever excesses may have accompanied it" (blah, blah) – for the heartlessness of the rich.

But one must not be too severe on dull-witted journalists, or on welfare workers who are "high" on Enlightened benevolence. The disastrous inference they make is only the inference which everyone around them makes. Malthus may have won the argument, but the anti-capitalists won everything else. It was the revolutionary Thomas Paine who proposed

---

* For related discussion, see D. C. Stove, "Why You Should Be a Conservative," in *On Enlightenment*, pp. 171–78. – Ed.

the system, and the level, of taxation under which we actually live. It was the revolutionary socialists Margaret Sanger and Emma Goldman, two of the bourgeois family's fiercest enemies, who converted America and then the world to contraception.[49] The man who tested homemade bombs for some of his political friends, and coined the word "secularism" for his own position, G. J. Holyoake, was a complete embodiment of the religion and politics of a century later.[50] Havelock Ellis, who did more than any other man to Enlighten our sexual lives (though himself childless, impotent, and indeed without any sexual interests except in women urinating) was also the man who invented the National Health Service of Britain.[51] And so on.

"We are all socialists nowadays," said the future King Edward VII in 1895.* It was true, even then. It is far more true now – far more deeply rooted, not only in our minds, but in our characters – than it was then.

* * *

Let me summarize what I have said so far in this section. The dismantling of the welfare state, or even any significant reduction in its size, is not going to happen for three reasons: because it is electorally impossible, at least while universal suffrage, or any close approach to it, exists; because the welfare state has a built-in tendency to increase in size, and there is nothing in sight capable of counteracting that tendency;

* The remark was made in a speech at Mansion House on November 5, 1895, when he was Prince of Wales; it echoed the remark "We are all socialists now" made years earlier by Sir William Harcourt. – Ed.

and because Enlightened benevolence, which first brought the welfare state into being, is far more intense and widespread now than it ever was before.

* * *

Since about 1920, three factors have combined to "cushion," counterbalance, and even outweigh the poverty generated by the welfare state. One of these factors corresponds to the high child mortality in workhouses, which Malthus pointed out as cushioning the effects of the Poor Laws; this is the enormous increase, in the last seventy years, of the practice of contraception.

The other two factors are the petrol engine and industrial electricity. These two things, which both date from about 1890 but only began to "tell" in the 1920s, have together effected an economic revolution compared with which "the industrial revolution" of the nineteenth century was no more than a feeble joke.* For they have made all agriculture, industry, distribution of goods, transport of persons, and domestic work incomparably more efficient and more painless than they ever were before.

Given the increased wealth which petrol and electricity

---

* For example, the first electric trams in England appeared in Blackpool in 1885; Edison and Swan together produced the first commercial electric lamps in the United States in 1887; Westinghouse began the manufacturing of electric motors in 1888; Diesel patented his internal-combustion engine in 1892; Ford built his first car in 1893; and the first industrial hydroelectric plant at Niagara Falls opened for business in 1896. For related discussion, see D. C. Stove, "A Promise Kept by Accident," in *On Enlightenment*, pp. 27–45. – Ed.

brought about, there was nothing unpredictable about the increase in contraception, for lessened fertility is a usual effect of increased prosperity. But the arrival of the petrol engine and electricity themselves, on the other hand, and still more their arrival together, was an event as absolutely unpredictable as any in history. An entirely new form of energy, easily adapted to perform a thousand different kinds of work, and soon cheaply available to almost everyone: there had never previously been even one such thing in the whole history of the world, let alone two of them at once.

It is difficult now to take in the fact – and yet it is a fact – that countries like Britain, America, and Australia, at the time (around 1875) when they began to become welfare states, were still economies of the same primitive kind as every earlier human economy had been. That is, they depended for most of their energy on one tiny and now-irrelevant source: the muscles of humans and animals. What the economic result would have been if they had *remained* muscle econ - omies, while the whole weight of Enlightened benevolence descended on them, is a question which we need not resort to a thought experiment to answer. The answer is obvious, both from general considerations and from the example of Russia since 1917. There have also, of course, been many subsequent examples of the effect of imposing Enlightened benevolence on a primitive economy.

Just when, therefore, communist governments actually spread for a time from Russia to Germany, Austria, and Hungary, and just when almost the entire world was united in expecting capitalism to join slavery and feudalism in the museum of history, the welfare states in fact began to enjoy unprecedented wealth. The communists were as much taken by surprise as everyone else. Late in his life, Lenin was obliged to "discover" that communism equals soviet power plus electrification, even at the cost of implying that Karl Marx had not known the half of it about communism; which he hardly could have, since industrial electricity did not exist when he died in 1883.

Whether petrol and electricity have *prevented* the welfare states from going over Niagara, or have merely postponed that event, is more than any rational person will claim to know. On the other hand, we *do* know that the welfare state and communism both stem from the same psychological root, namely Enlightened benevolence, and that *that* current of feeling is actually stronger now than it ever has been before. We also know that the inherent tendency of the welfare state is to increase poverty; that "welfare" still continues every year to absorb a greater proportion of our nations' wealth and population; and that there is no social force in sight which is capable of stopping that process. Of course we *may* be saved again by another energy revolution, like the one which petrol and electricity effected; but the intrinsic improbability of that is against it, and there is no positive evidence whatever in its favor.

IF THE WELFARE state is irreversible, the prospect of communism being dismantled must be more remote still. You cannot build a boat in the waters at the foot of Niagara. It is easy, by breaking eggs, to make an omelette; but who knows how to make eggs out of omelettes?

Even if anyone knew how to do it, it could not be done if there were hardly any omelette left. Fifty years of communism is not just fifty years of the non-creation of wealth: it is also fifty years of the destruction of pre-communist wealth. This is a loss which it can scarcely be possible to make up. Yet at present everyone talks, not only in the communist states but in the free countries as well, as though the communist countries now, in 1989, have a reasonable economic basis from which to start, and only need to make sensible political decisions in order to build satisfactorily upon it.

Last week, for example, the government of Hungary astonished us all by announcing, in effect, that in the future that country would become a welfare, as distinct from a communist, state.* That is, that there would be far more wealth,

* In February 1989, a Central Committee plenum gave in-principle endorsement to the adoption of a multiparty political system. Between June

99

and far less terror, than in its communist past. Alas, beggars *cannot* be choosers. As Malthus insisted, wealth can never be increased, however little, by any *"fiat* of government." The actual welfare states owe their wealth partly to such inherited wealth as they have allowed to survive death duties, but principally to taxing the income which capitalist energy still generates day by day. Of course they despise and condemn and harass this goose which lays golden eggs for them; but at least they *have* such a goose. Hungary, and every other communist country, has none. They once did, but they killed it.

But the most important consideration is not the communist countries' actual poverty. It is their wholesale extinction of those elements in human psychology that *can* create wealth. If the dosages of Enlightened benevolence which we in the West have absorbed are high enough to impose colossal burdens on our economic life, they are still nothing by comparison with the dosages which the citizens of communist countries have absorbed. The root of the trouble with the

---

and September 1989, the Communist Party then held roundtable talks on the possibility of transforming Hungary into a democratic state. The talks, chaired by the Speaker of Parliament, Mátyás Szűrös, produced an agreement in principle between the ruling Hungarian Socialist Workers' Party and various opposition groups. Hungary's constitution was revised shortly afterwards, on October 18, 1989. Five days later, on the anniversary of the 1956 Revolution, the Hungarian People's Republic ceased to exist and the new Hungarian Republic officially came into being. The Berlin Wall fell seventeen days later, on November 9, setting the stage for the signing of the "two plus four" treaty on September 12, 1990. This treaty, signed by the four great powers (the United Kingdom, the United States, France, and the Soviet Union) as well as the two Germanies brought to an official end the rights of the Allied powers and restored full sovereignty to the German people. The official reunification of Germany took place less than a month later, on October 3, 1990. – Ed.

welfare states, and what makes them irreversible, is (as I said) us: the citizens. The same is true, only much more so, of the citizens of communist states.

Of course millions of those citizens now assure us that they are thoroughly disillusioned with communism. These assurances are undoubtedly sincere, but I venture to believe that they are mistaken. What these citizens *are* thoroughly disillusioned with is poverty and coercion; but they are not psychologically ready to part with free education, or health care, or old-age pensions, or workers' compensation. Even we are not, as I have said, and on present evidence we never will be. Still less can they be. Like us, only more so, these citizens (very naturally) want the benefits of Enlightened benevolence without its costs: the welfare state maximized, without poverty and terror. But this is wanting to have a certain cause while being free from its effects.

At the moment I write this, the economy of post-communist Poland is sustained only by money from Western governments; but this can hardly be a pattern for any real economic recovery from communism. It simply means that the welfare states have taken on their largest welfare client ever: the population of Poland. But even the wealth of Japan could not long sustain *Russia*, for example, as a part of its welfare program.

The truths which Malthus vainly strove to impart cannot be too often repeated. These are that widespread poverty *cannot* be relieved from the outside and, therefore, can be relieved (if at all) only by the industry, self-reliance, and prudence of the poor themselves. But the worldwide triumph of Enlightened benevolence has been at the expense of precisely these traits of character. Indeed, it has even made their *names* objects of disgust, as I said earlier, and this is where these words are understood at all, for it's likely that half the present voters in the welfare states have never so much as *heard* these words in their lives. Nowadays, a politician at election time might just as well deplore "imdrupence" as deplore imprudence; either way, at least half of his listeners would not have the faintest idea what he was talking about.

As well as poverty, another thing always arrives wherever communism does, and as soon as it does: terror. Without terror, communist poverty must be even worse than it is with terror. Where nothing else remains to put a spring in the collective farmer's step, terror can. So since I believe, for the reasons given in the last few pages, that communist *poverty* is irreversible, I predict that terror will soon resume its accustomed position in those communist countries which have lately relaxed it to a greater or lesser degree. Of course it will be extremely unwelcome to the vast majority of citizens. But what of that? It always was, but that was never sufficient to prevent it.

XII

THE DIFFERENCE to the world which Enlightened benevolence has made is a huge and undeniable fact. Yet it is also a puzzling fact. The Enlightenment's ideal of the benevolent man is so remote from reality and so unattractive: how can it have transformed the world?

It is quite different with, say, the Christian ideal of the saint, or the military ideal of the warrior. We all know of real examples of those ideals, or at least can form a mental picture of one; and they are ideals which evoke some spontaneous response in every human heart. But the benevolent man of the Enlightenment evokes no such response; and anyway, there never really was anyone whose benevolence was completely universal, disinterested, and external, as Enlightened benevolence is required to be. If we try to form a mental picture of a man of *Enlightened* benevolence, we are likely to find ourselves picturing an eighteenth-century wig, and nothing else.

If, however, we relax the Enlightenment requirements slightly and try to form simply the mental image of a *benevolent* man – without the characteristics of universality, disinterestedness, and externality – then a picture comes easily enough to mind. (At least, it does with me, and I do not think this is a matter of idiosyncrasy.) The benevolent man is past middle age, rich, cheerful, popular, a bachelor or a widower with no living children of his own, retired from active life of any kind, if indeed he ever took part in it, with nothing much to do, except be benevolent.

This picture has several interesting features. First, it has to be a picture of a man. Women cannot quite rise to the dignity of *abstract* benevolence; the reason being, I suppose, that they are much too likely to be engaged in some *particular* exercise of affection, sympathy, or usefulness. Second, it is evidently a picture of a man whose passions are weaker, and whose points of attachment to normal human life are fewer, than those of most men. Third, even though we deliberately did not require him to be *Enlightened*-benevolent, he still has an overpowering unreality about him. There never was such a person, and never will be.

Even if there were, who could possibly feel any spontaneous enthusiasm for him? Surely only people who are *themselves* deficient in feeling, and have few attachments by way of blood, marriage, or occupation to normal human life? Only people, in other words, like Voltaire, Hume, Gibbon, Bentham, and J. S. Mill: men whose lives were, almost without remainder, *their writings*.

The very words "benevolence" and "benevolent" are exclusively *writers'* words, and have been so for three hundred years. They have never taken root in English speech; they occur almost nowhere except in print. From the passage of Hume which was quoted in section III above, we learn that it was people "in *speculative* life" who had lately begun praising benevolence so much. In the twentieth century no one, even those of us who *are* in speculative life, would ever say that such-and-such a person is benevolent. We would say that he or she is "patient and kind and generous to everyone," or something like that; anyway, never "benevolent." Of course in a novel like Holcroft's *Anna St. Ives* (1795), the excruciatingly Enlightened heroine talks a lot about benevolence; and no doubt Holcroft himself, in conversations with such friends as Godwin and Mary Wollstonecraft, often used the word; but this only confirms my generalization, that the word has never been used at all outside print, except by writers.

Of all the people we ourselves have met, who are the ones that have been most deeply influenced by the Enlightenment ideal of benevolence? Why, of course, those hardened Communist Party functionaries who, between about 1930 and 1976,* devoted their lives to running the Teachers' Federation, the Postal Workers' Union, or whatever it might be. The type is much less common now, perhaps even extinct; but at the time, it was often observed that such people had something very parched and cold about them. The *future* happiness of the workers was the only subject at all capable of warming them into any enthusiasm. Their *actual* feelings towards *actual* workers, especially if the latter showed any signs of *present* happiness, were generally not benevolent at all, but rather (to speak plainly) murderous. These communists used to imitate Christ at least in this, that they never

* The year 1930 marked the beginning of the Great Depression, following the stock market crash of October 1929. The year 1976 marked the reunification of Vietnam under communist rule following the end of the Vietnam War. – Ed.

laughed;[52] and, in the 1920s, visitors to Russia who had first visited it before 1917 often remarked upon the utter disappearance of laughter from Russian life.

* * *

So to repeat: how *can* an ideal so unreal and so unattractive have produced so much change in the world? I do not know. I merely insist that both sides of the paradox are true: that Enlightened benevolence is unreal, and has no attraction except for a few cold-blooded people who exist on the margins of normal life, *and* that it rules our world.

Is BENEVOLENCE a virtue at all? I do not say that it is not, but anyone who thinks it self-evident that it *is* a virtue needs to be reminded of certain facts: facts both of logic and of history.

First, the logical facts. Your benevolence, or lack of it, is *entirely* a matter of your disposition of mind, of what you are, on balance, disposed to do. If you are, on balance, disposed to make X happier than X otherwise would have been, then you are benevolently disposed towards X; and conversely. That is all there is to benevolence towards X.

The *actual effect* on X, of anything which your benevolent disposition may lead you to do, does not come into it. Your action may fail to affect X at all, or it may even decrease his happiness; but as long as your action issued from a disposition to increase X's happiness, then you acted benevolently. Nor does it make any difference what *beliefs* you may have as to what would make X happier. If you have false beliefs on that subject then you are more likely to act in a way which fails to increase X's happiness, or which actually decreases it; but as long as you remain disposed to increase X's happiness, it remains true that your disposition towards him is a benevolent one.

Benevolence is not even inconsistent with any number of acts of cruelty inflicted on the objects of one's benevolence. Peter the Great, for example, was guilty of many acts of atrocious cruelty to some of his subjects; but there is not the slightest reason to doubt that his Enlightened efforts to introduce Western science and technology into Russia were prompted, at least in part, by a benevolent intention to alleviate his subjects' poverty.

Suppose, then, that my benevolence towards X leads me to do something which, through ill luck or mistaken beliefs about what would increase X's happiness, in fact makes X unhappier. In such a case, it is mere confusion of thought to say that I did not *really* act benevolently, or that I acted only *would-be* benevolently, or only *benevolently-by-my-own-lights*. In the case as described, I *acted benevolently*, or out of benevolence – full stop. It was just that things did not turn out as I had intended.

Now, some historical facts. For example, there is the fact that Joseph Stalin was a man of very enlarged benevolence. He was disposed, on balance, to make X happier than X otherwise would have been, where X was "all future human beings, and all present ones who are not friends of the institution of private property." He was not simply disposed *on balance* that way: the disposition in him was very strong, at least when he was young. It was strong enough, at any rate, to carry him out of the seminary and into the arduous life of a revolutionary agitator.

Stalin's benevolence did not prevent him from inflicting extreme cruelty on many people, a large proportion of whom were among the objects of his benevolence, but this combination is not logically anomalous, as I have just pointed out, and it is not even, in fact, uncommon. Unlike Stalin, Al Capone was not an Enlightened man and his benevolence was not nearly so enlarged; but he displayed much more benevolence than most of us ever do. That is one difference between Capone and most of us. Another difference is that he sometimes found it easy to beat people to death using a baseball bat, or to shoot them in cold blood. These differences are both simply facts. They are not even especially interesting facts, except to the extent that they teach us not to think about benevolence in a way which would imply the impossibility of such facts.

Stalin had certain false beliefs, of course, about what would increase human happiness, especially the belief that community of property would bring about an immense increase of happiness; but then, as we have seen, this belief had been shared for nearly two hundred years by very many of the most Enlightened and benevolent people of Europe. (It still is.) Stalin's benevolence, combined with this false belief, led him to do many things which were, of course, enormously destructive of happiness. But again, as we have also seen, neither an unhappy outcome nor the influence of false beliefs about how to increase happiness makes a man's benevolent actions any the less benevolent.

Though it is a simple historical fact that Stalin was a benevolent man, it may be asking too much of the reader to expect him to reconcile himself at once to this fact. So let us change the example. Consider instead two people who bore, after all, far more responsibility for the Eastern Bloc's tumbling over Niagara than did Stalin: Karl Marx and Vladimir Ilyich Lenin.

Marx's *Capital* (1867) pretends to be a work of science and of sober economic history, but this pretense is so transparent that it could scarcely deceive an intelligent child of nine. The book is simply one of the hundreds of literary explosions by Enlightened and benevolent people of the nineteenth century writing about "the social problem," "the deplorable condition of the working class," etc., etc. That is, *Capital* belongs to exactly the same species of literature, as well as to the same decade, as Charles Kingsley's *The Water Babies* (1863).

Capital is an appeal to our hearts about the working class in general. *The Water Babies* is an appeal to our hearts about the particular case of child chimney sweeps. No one denies the obvious fact that Kingsley wrote his book with a benevolent intention, or the fact that the book actually had some of its intended effect: the laws protecting child chimney sweeps were strengthened the very next year. Nor should anyone deny the obvious fact that Marx wrote *his* book with a benevolent intention, even though, far from having its intended effect, it has caused the most stupendous amount of misery.

Lenin, of course, was an altogether different character type. In Marx we can still recognize a human being: an extremely dangerous and disagreeable one, but still a human being. Even at that, we also recognize a benevolent one, since there cannot be the slightest doubt that Marx was strongly disposed to increase the future happiness of the human race. In contrast, Lenin was one of the first post-people people, whom communism later spawned in incalculable numbers.

Benevolence was still, indeed, the ruling passion with him, but it was that *Enlightened* benevolence, which – as I said in the preceding section – many of us have actually met in his political descendants: parched, cold, murderous, without actually being cruel. (To those who experienced the effects of Lenin's benevolence, cruelty from him would have been a relief: a reassuring touch of common humanity.) His was the benevolence of a *marginal* man. He had no child, no home, no property, no occupation even, until the chance came to inaugurate his reign of benevolence on earth. Up to and including late 1916, Lenin never had a present, only a future; but then came, out of the blue and through none of his doing, help and a huge sum of money from the German High Command.[53] And Lenin all at once acquired a present – and Russia lost its future!

XIV

"WHAT DO YOU want your child to be?" Parents are often asked this question, or ask it of themselves, when their children are babies, or about to be born. The question is asked less often as the babies grow up, because parents gradually discover that what they want has very little to do with what their children are to be. But while the question still is being asked, the answer which is almost always given to it, nowadays at least, is this: "As long as they're happy! That's all that really matters, isn't it?"

Well, that is exactly what the Enlightenment had always said, of course; not about individual babies, but about future humanity at large. That, after all, had been the whole *point* of dismantling religion, democratizing government, equalizing wealth, emancipating women, and all the rest of it. All those things simply were the means to a single end: that people in the future should be happy. "That's all that really matters, isn't it?"

When parents nowadays give the conventional answer, it is almost certain that their doing so is itself an effect of the Enlightenment. It is not the answer which would have first occurred to a Spartan parent in 450 BC, for example, or to a

Calvinist parent in 1580 AD. But even if everyone *had* always said that happiness is the only thing that matters, it would still be a stupid thing to say, either about our babies' lives or about the future of the human race.

Your baby boy may turn out to be an idiot who is always extremely happy. Would you still say then that happiness is all that matters to you about his life? Or he may grow into a man who can be happy only by raping every woman he can reach and who, favored by fortune, in fact leads a supremely happy life. Would the spectacle of his life make you happy then?

Your daughter, yet unborn, might turn out to be a conjoined twin. If it further turned out that she is a *happy* conjoined twin, would you still say that her life had everything that matters? Or it may turn out that, though your daughter is physically normal, her sole idea of happiness is permanent invalidism. If her life actually provided her with this source of happiness, would that be all that mattered to you?

This happy though permanently invalid daughter might even be on the right track, at that, and be a pointer to the way ahead for the whole human race. When our medical technology becomes a little more advanced, it might turn out that the way for a human being to be happiest is to be kept permanently in a hospital bottle, with the brain suitably stimulated by chemical or electrical means. All the pleasures of normal life, and none of the pains, might be experienced in this way, even though the "life" being led is entirely hallucinatory. If this option became medically possible, would you still say that your child's happiness is all that matters?

If that option *did* become available, then of course the axioms of the Enlightenment would prescribe unmistakably that as many people as possible should live in this way. The axiom of the greatest happiness of the greatest number could be satisfied by nothing else. Of course the accommodation problem would be severe, but at least it could be alleviated – since a body is obviously inessential for the kind of life in question – by keeping only the *brain* in the bottle. Bearing in mind the first epigraph to the present essay, and in memory of the greatest enemy to human unhappiness which our race has known, the bottles should be called "Lenin bottles."

Here, then, is a way in which it might prove to be possible to realize in practice all the axioms and theorems of the Enlightenment, and to satisfy the age-old yearning of humanity for happiness. There would be no more war or cruelty or inequality, no more oppression of the workers, or of women or blacks, no more fox hunting . . . just maximum happiness. If it is true that happiness is all that matters, then this form of utopia is entitled to our most earnest consideration. Of course it is, for technical reasons, only a remote possibility at present, but it need not always remain so. Suppose it did become feasible: what objection to this way of life could an *Enlightened* person consistently make?

THE DESIRE to relieve the suffering of our fellows, Malthus says, is as natural as our desires for food and drink. It is not as strong, and not as universal, as those desires are; still, it is very widespread and, in many people, it is strong. It further resembles our desires for food and drink in this way: it is a desire easily overindulged, and when its over-indulgence is inveterate, the results are disastrous.[54] All of this is profoundly true; but it actually understates the case. The whole of economic history since 1789 testifies that, the more extravagantly you indulge your benevolence, the more extravagant still will your next indulgence of it need to be. Benevolence is the heroin of the Enlightened.

I believe I can explain the extreme ease with which benevolence runs to overindulgence. It is due to a certain asymmetry in human nature. We have a virtually infinite capacity to absorb the love, kind treatment, and good opinion of others; but we have a very limited capacity to absorb their hatred, ill treatment, or contempt, or even their mere neglect.

It was a profound remark which T. H. Huxley somewhere made that not even the greatest philosopher, saint, or sage is entirely indifferent to the scorn of even the merest street urchin.* There are very few of us who can maintain our self-respect without the respect of at least *some* others, and a person who has lost *all* self-respect is, quite literally, in danger of his life, even without the attentions of his personal enemies or the public authorities.

But who, on the other hand, ever had *too much* positive attention, praise, kind regard, or love? An Augustus or Joseph Stalin may, occasionally, feel a slight tinge of nausea from a surfeit of those things; still, he will soon get over it. The rest of us will never get a chance to learn whether *we* would be any more easily surfeited! Even in a small and economically unimportant class of people there can be titanic energies at work demanding praise or love. The vanity of authors is an example: if it could be efficiently harnessed, it would end the world's energy shortage overnight.

This asymmetry in our nature is so extremely obvious that no one can ever have been entirely ignorant of it. But it is of a fearful depth, which has hardly ever been looked into; and, as a result, its consequences have never been thought out. If they had been, we could have been able to *predict in advance*, for example, that the health care of one man, if he could exact all the medical attention he might like, would be enough to exhaust the treasury of the entire National Health Service. Not predicting this, we had to wait to learn it from painful experience instead.

This asymmetry in us is evidently a consequence of our being one of the *social* animals, for it is more pronounced still

---

* T. H. Huxley, *Aphorisms and Reflections* (London: Macmillan & Co., 1907), §CCXXXIII, p. 97. – Ed.

in those animals which are even more social than we are. An unpopular ant or bee, for example, or even one which has accidentally acquired the odor of a foreign community, is simply a dead ant or bee, even more quickly than his human counterpart was in Stalin's Russia or Capone's Chicago. By contrast, cats (for example) absorb both the antagonism and the affability of other cats without any discernible effect on their own equanimity, let alone on their prospects of survival.

It might have been supposed that this asymmetry contains, in itself, the seeds of enough human misery to go on with; but no, there is something else in us (and, again, in all the social animals) which comes in to augment it. This is a certain "polar wind" principle which drives unhappiness to accumulate most where most unhappiness exists already; and likewise for happiness.

If an urchin screams his derision at a passing sage, he not only decreases, however slightly, the sage's well-being: he significantly increases the probability that a second urchin will do the same. Two screaming urchins make it much more probable still that a third urchin will scream ... and so on. *To him that hath contempt, even more contempt shall be given.** A bird who lives in a community of his conspecifics may find one day that he is at the bottom of the social scale, and he may therefore imagine that things cannot get any worse from then on. He is mistaken: not because you can go any lower than the bottom, but because, by a little ingenuity higher up, tomorrow's bottom always can be pushed even lower than

* Cf. Matthew 13:12 and Luke 19:25. – Ed.

today's. King Lear, brought low, was barked at by his own dogs.*

Just as unhappiness accumulates at the unhappiness-pole, so happiness accumulates at the happiness-pole. Nothing succeeds like success. If Sir V.W. or Professor X.Y. is appointed this year to a profitable and non-onerous position on the board of company A, then, short of divine intervention to prevent it, he will be appointed next year to a similar position on the board of company B as well. It is nature's law; and in this respect the rich are *not* different from us, as Scott Fitzgerald said they were.† Whoever you are, and whomever you meet, you cannot smile at them the first time without at least making it more probable that you will smile at them the next time.

* * *

Now, put together three facts about the human race. First, there is the asymmetry that I have just mentioned: that our absorption capacity for care is virtually infinite, while our absorption capacity for its opposite, or even its absence, is low. Second, there is the "polar wind" principle: that unhappiness is bound to accumulate most where most unhappiness exists already; and likewise for happiness. Third, there is the fact mentioned at the start of this essay: that the sources of our unhappiness are inexhaustibly various.

---

* William Shakespeare, *King Lear*, act III, scene VI. – Ed.

† F. Scott Fitzgerald, *The Crack-Up*, ed. E. Wilson (New York: New Directions, 1956), p. 25. Cf. Ernest Hemingway, *The Snows of Kilimanjaro and Other Stories* (New York: Charles Scribner's Sons, 1927), p. 23. – Ed.

Is this a *promising* combination of facts? Is a species that satisfies these three descriptions one which is separated from universal happiness only by a few, or accidental, obstacles? While these descriptions remained true of us, could anyone rationally expect to make us happy by changing only our external circumstances?

Yet it is this species, according to the Enlightenment, which not only is perfectly capable of universal happiness, but has so far been denied it only by certain ridiculous, or rather insane, historical accidents;[55] by such accidents, that is, as the inequality of wealth, the vainglory of kings, the madness or the cunning of priests, the precedence which men have arrogated to themselves over women. The Enlightenment, accordingly, set about the removal of those obstacles; and it has very largely succeeded in removing them all.

Alas, not only did universal happiness not result, a monstrous crop of entirely new evils sprang up. When wealth was equalized in the only way that can make such equality permanent – by the abolition of private property – unprecedented poverty and unprecedented terror descended upon Russia. When bourgeois marriage was discredited everywhere – and in America at present, for example, half of all marriages end in divorce – then at least half of every generation of children became exposed to a source of intense misery which previously had hardly existed. When the virtue of filial piety was laughed out of existence, another utterly new element was added to human misery: care of the aged by public institutions alone, and so on.

XVI

THERE IS A story in American literature somewhere, but I cannot remember where, of a solitary Indian in his canoe, who has been fishing many miles upstream from Niagara Falls.* Despite all his local knowledge, he makes some slight misjudgment of time, or wind, or water, and finds himself surprised by the current. For hours he puts forth all his strength in trying to reach the shore, but long before the fatal event itself, he passes a point at which his diminishing strength, and the increasing strength of the current, make further resistance vain. He then ships his paddle, lights his pipe, and folds his arms.

In the circumstances, those are the actions of a rational man. Similarly, in my opinion, the world-current of Enlightened benevolence is now so strong, and we have been launched upon it for so many years, that we passed the point of no return a long time ago, and will, if we are rational, emulate the Indian in the story.†

* The story is recounted in Louis Albert Banks, *The Fisherman and His Friends* (New York: Funk & Wagnalls, 1896), pp. 335–36. – Ed.

† Five years after writing these words, in June 1994 after being treated for cancer, David Stove took his own life. – Ed.

A BIBLIOGRAPHY OF
D. C. (DAVID CHARLES) STOVE
AND RELATED WRITINGS

COMPILED BY

JAMES FRANKLIN, ANDREW IRVINE,

SCOTT CAMPBELL, AND SELMAN HALABI

Inactive internet links often may be found
archived at The Internet Archive,
www.archive.org

A. BOOKS

Probability and Hume's Inductive Scepticism.
Oxford: Clarendon Press, 1973.

REVIEWS

S. Blackburn, "Past Certainties and Future Possibilities," *Times Literary Supplement*, 3727 (August 10, 1973), 935; discussed in J. L. Mackie and S. Blackburn, "Hume and Induction," *Times Literary Supplement*, 3734 (September 28, 1973), 1133; and J. L. Mackie and S. Blackburn, "Hume and Induction," *Times Literary Supplement*, 3736 (October 12, 1973), 1234; with Stove's reply in "Hume, Induction and the Irish" (1976).

Bibliography

J. Janssens, in *Tijdschrift voor Filosofie*, 35 (1973), 646–647.

A. Flew, in *Philosophical Quarterly*, 24 (1974), 72–73.

I. M. Fowlie, in *Philosophical Books*, 15:2 (May 1974), 24–26.

I. Hinckfuss, in *Australasian Journal of Philosophy*, 52 (1974), 269–276; with Stove's reply in "Hume, Induction and the Irish" (1976).

A. C. Michalos, in *Philosophia*, 4 (1974), 375–379.

J. F. Fox, in *British Journal for the Philosophy of Science*, 26 (1975), 85–87.

C. A. Hooker, in *Hume Studies*, 1 (1975), 25–29.

D. W. Livingston, in *Journal of the History of Philosophy*, 13 (1975), 413–415.

M. Williams, in *Philosophical Review*, 84 (1975), 453–457.

E. Millstone, in *Mind*, 85 (1976), 297–298.

R. George, in *Canadian Journal of Philosophy*, 7 (1977), 203–211.

DISCUSSION AND CITATION

J. E. Adler, "Stove on Hume's Inductive Scepticism," *Australasian Journal of Philosophy*, 53 (1975), 167–170; with Stove's reply in "Hume, Induction and the Irish" (1976).

S. Waterlow, "On a Proposed Refutation of Hume," *Analysis*, 36 (1975), 43–46.

P. J. McGrath, "Hume's Inductive Scepticism," *Philosophical Studies* (Ireland), 24 (1976), 64–81.

J. Cassidy, "The Nature of Hume's Inductive Scepticism: A Critical Notice," *Ratio*, 19 (1977), 47–54.

B. Stroud, "Causality and the Inference from the Observed to the Unobserved: The Negative Phase," chap. 3 in *Hume* (London: Routledge & Kegan Paul, 1977), 42–67.

Bibliography

G. Gawlick, "Zwischen Empirismus und Skeptizismus," *Philosophische Rundschau*, 26 (1979), 161–186.

W. K. Goosens, "Stove and Inductive Scepticism," *Australasian Journal of Philosophy*, 57 (1979), 79–84.

J. Immerwahr, "A Skeptic's Progress: Hume's Preference for the First Enquiry," in *McGill Hume Studies*, ed. D. F. Norton, N. Capaldi, and W. L. Robison (San Diego: Austin Hill Press, 1979), 227–238.

D. M. Armstrong, *What Is a Law of Nature?* (Cambridge: Cambridge University Press, 1983), 57.

P. Engel, "Hume et le commencement de la philosophie," *Critique*, 39 (1983), 960–981.

K. Gemes, "A Refutation of Inductive Scepticism," *Australasian Journal of Philosophy*, 61 (1983), 434–438; repr. in *David Hume: Critical Assessments*, vol. 2, *Induction, Scepticism*, ed. S. Tweyman (London and New York: Routledge, 1995), 44–48.

S. A. Grave, *A History of Philosophy in Australia* (St. Lucia: University of Queensland Press, 1984), 192–193.

G. J. D. Moyal and S. Tweyman, *Early Modern Philosophy: Metaphysics, Epistemology, and Politics – Essays in Honour of Robert F. McRae* (Delmar, N.Y.: Caravan Books, 1986), 133.

B. Janz, "Reason, Inductive Inference, and True Religion in Hume," *Dialogue* (Canada), 27 (1988), 721–726.

W. E. Morris, "Hume's Refutation of Inductive Probabilism," in *Probability and Causality*, ed. J. H. Fetzer (Dordrecht and Boston: Reidel, 1988), 43–77.

C. Belshaw, "Scepticism and Madness," *Australasian Journal of Philosophy*, 67 (1989), 447–451.

R. J. Bench, "Paradigms, Methods and the Epistemology of Speech Pathology: Some Comments on Eastwood (1988)," *British Journal of Disorders of Communication*, 26 (1991), 235–242.

Bibliography

K. R. Merrill, "Hume's 'Of Miracles,' Peirce, and the Balancing of Likelihoods," *Journal of the History of Philosophy*, 29 (1991), 85–113.

A. W. Sparkes, *Talking Philosophy* (London and New York: Routledge, 1991), 288.

B. Maund, "History and Philosophy of Science in Australia," in *Essays on Philosophy in Australia*, ed. J. T. J. Srzednicki and D. Wood (Dordrecht, Boston, London: Kluwer, 1992), 243–46.

L. Cataldi Madonna, "Humes skeptisches Argument gegen die Vernunft," *Archiv für Geschichte der Philosophie*, 75 (1993), 179–194.

M. Levin, "Reliabilism and Induction," *Synthese*, 97 (1993), 297–334.

M. Markel, "Induction, Social Constructionism, and the Form of the Science Paper," *Journal of Technical Writing and Communication*, 23 (1993), 7–22.

A. Rosenberg, "Hume and the Philosophy of Science," in *The Cambridge Companion to Hume*, ed. D. F. Norton (Cambridge: Cambridge University Press, 1993), 77.

R. Niklaus, "Voltaire and English Empiricism," *Revue Internationale de Philosophie*, 48 (1994), 9–24.

P. J. R. Millican, "Hume's Argument Concerning Induction: Structure and Interpretation," in *David Hume: Critical Assessments*, vol. 2, *Induction, Scepticism*, ed. S. Tweyman (London and New York: Routledge, 1995), 91–144; repr. in *Hume: General Philosophy*, ed. D. W. D. Owen (Aldershot, UK: Ashgate, 2000), 165–218.

A. G. Padgett, "The Mutuality of Theology and Science: An Example from Time and Thermodynamics," *Christian Scholar's Review*, 26 (1996), 12–35; and online at www2.luthersem.edu/apadgett/mutuality.html

R. Weintraub, "The Sceptical Life," *Dialectica*, 50 (1996), 225–233.

Bibliography

L. Falkenstein, "Hume's Answer to Kant," *Noûs*, 32 (1998), 331–360.

R. Lantin, "Hume and the Problem of Induction," *Philosophia*, 26:1–2 (1998), 105–117.

A. Mura, "Hume's Inductive Logic," *Synthese*, 115 (1998), 303–331.

J. Greco, "Agent Reliabilism," *Philosophical Perspectives*, 13 (1999), 273–296.

J. Greco, "Hume's Skepticism about Unobserved Matters of Fact," chap. 6 in *Putting Skeptics in Their Place* (Cambridge: Cambridge University Press, 2000), 137–163.

B. K. Hinton, "Is Hume's Inductive Skepticism Based upon *Rationalistic Assumptions?*" *Modern Schoolman*, 77 (2000), 309–332.

K. Meeker, "Hume's Iterative Probability Argument: A Pernicious Reductio," *Journal of the History of Philosophy*, 38 (2000), 221–238.

S. Hetherington, "Why There Need Not Be Any Grue Problem about Inductive Inference as Such," *Philosophy*, 76 (2001), 127–136.

M. Huemer, "The Problem of Defeasible Justification," *Erkenntnis*, 54 (2001), 375–397.

S. Okasha, "Verificationism, Realism and Scepticism," *Erkenntnis*, 55 (2001), 371–385.

S. Okasha, "What Did Hume Really Show about Induction?" *Philosophical Quarterly*, 51 (2001), 307–327.

A. Bailey, *First Philosophy: Fundamental Problems and Readings in Philosophy* (Peterborough, Ontario: Broadview Press, 2002), 280.

D. Murdoch, "Induction, Hume, and Probability," *Journal of Philosophy*, 99 (2002), 185–199.

Bibliography

J. Franklin, *Corrupting the Youth* (Sydney: Macleay Press, 2003), 438.

M. Levin, "Reliabilism and Induction," in *Philosophical Skepticism*, ed. C. Landesman and R. Meeks (Oxford: Blackwell, 2003), 163–164.

H. Beebee, *Hume on Causation* (New York: Routledge, 2006), 20.

Popper and After: Four Modern Irrationalists.
   Oxford: Pergamon, 1982.

    CONTENTS
    Preface
    Part One: Philosophy and the English Language –
      How Irrationalism about Science Is Made Credible
      1. Neutralising Success-words
      2. Sabotaging Logical Expressions
    Part Two: How Irrationalism about Science Began
      3. The Historical Source Located
      4. The Key Premise of Irrationalism Identified
      5. Further Evidence for This Identification
    Notes
    Bibliography
    Index

TRANSLATION

Popper y Después. Translated by Susana Nuccetelli. Madrid: Tecnos, 1995.

REVISED EDITIONS

Anything Goes: Origins of the Cult of Scientific Irrationalism. With a Foreword by Keith Windschuttle and an Afterword by James Franklin. Paddington, NSW: Macleay Press, 1998.

Bibliography

Scientific Irrationalism: Origins of a Postmodern Cult. With a
Foreword by Keith Windschuttle and an Afterword by James
Franklin. New Brunswick, N.J., and London: Transaction
Publishers, 2001.

REVIEWS

J. Largeault, in *Revue Philosophique de la France et de l'étranger*, 108
(1983), 369–371.

M. Levin, in *Quadrant*, 27:6 (June 1983), 80–81.

A. Lugg, in *Philosophy of Science*, 50 (1983), 350–352.

D. Papineau, "The Irrationalist Conspiracy," *Times Literary Supplement*, 4187 (July 1, 1983), 693.

M. Bunge, in *New Ideas in Psychology*, 2 (1984), 81–82.

R. Fellows, in *Philosophical Books*, 25 (1984), 250–252.

J. F. Fox, in *Australasian Journal of Philosophy*, 62 (1984), 99–101.

J. M. B. Moss, in *British Journal for the Philosophy of Science*, 35
(1984), 307–310.

R. Temple, "A Major Threat to Rationality," *New Scientist*, 1393
(January 19, 1984), 36.

J. Agassi, in *Philosophy of the Social Sciences*, 15 (1985), 368–369.

B. Baertschi, in *Studia Philosophica* (Switzerland), 44 (1985),
237–239.

J. R. Brown, in *Dialogue* (Canada), 24 (1985), 177–179.

M. Hammersley, "The Good, the Bad, and the Gullible," *British
Journal of Sociology of Education*, 6 (1985), 243–248.

J. M. Brown, in *Philosophical Studies* (Ireland), 31 (1986/1987),
356–361.

K. Jodkowski, in *Zagadnienia Naukoznawstwa*, 23:1 (1987),
119–127.

Bibliography

S. Campbell, "Irrational Philosophy," *The Skeptic* (UK), 12:3–4 (1999), 45.

S. Campbell, "Stove Applies Heat to Popper," *The Skeptic* (Australia), 19:3 (Spring 1999), 38–39.

D. Carlyle and N. Walker, in *The Australian*, January 6, 1999, 29; discussed in R. Blackford, "The Left's Defection from Progress," *Quadrant*, 43:4 (April 1999), 47–52.

M. Charlesworth, "Enfant Terrible?" *Australian Book Review*, 211 (June 1999), 13.

S. Goode, "Essays from an Australian Philosopher and Wit," *Washington Times*, February 27, 2000, B7.

T. S. Hibbs, "Heat and Light," *Weekly Standard*, 6:2 (September 18, 2000), 27–29.

J. J. C. Smart, in *Australasian Journal of Philosophy*, 81 (2003), 429–433.

DISCUSSION AND CITATION

P. Engel, "Hume et le commencement de la philosophie," *Critique*, 39 (1983), 960–981.

Z. A. Sokuler, "Several Trends and Problems in Contemporary Western Philosophical Science," *Voprosy Filosofii*, 11 (1983), 123–133.

J. R. Kantor, "Scientific Unity and Spiritistic Disunity," *Psychological Record*, 34 (1984), 69–71.

R. Sylvan, "Science and Science: Relocating Stove and the Modern Irrationalist," *Research Series in Unfashionable Philosophy*, 1 (1984), 35–54; transl. P. Giza as "Nauka a nauka: ponowne umiejscowienie Stove' a i wspolczesnych irracjonalistow," in *Realizm, Racjonalnosc, Relatywizm*, vol. 7 (Lublin: MCS Publishing House, 1991), 133–149.

K. Hegland, "Goodbye to Deconstruction," *Southern California Law Review*, 58 (1985), 1216–1219.

Bibliography

J. Watkins, "On Stove's Book, by a Fifth 'Irrationalist'," *Austral-asian Journal of Philosophy*, 63 (1985), 259–268; transl. J. Wozniak as "Piaty 'irracjonalista' o ksiazce Stove' a," in *Realiẓm, Racjonal-nosc, Relatywiẓm*, vol. 7 (Lublin: MCS Publishing House, 1991), 151–164.

T. Theocharis and M. Psimopolous, "Where Science Has Gone Wrong," *Nature*, 6140 (October 15, 1987), 595–598.

A. Garrett, "Popperism" (letter), *The Skeptic* (Australia), 7:1 (Autumn 1987), 19.

R. H. Popkin and C. B. Schmitt, *Scepticism from the Renaissance to the Enlightenment* (n.p.: Harrassowitz, 1987), 184.

S. Yates, "Stove's *Critique* of 'Irrationalists'," *Metaphilosophy*, 18 (1987), 149–160.

D. Dutton, "Bookmarks," *Philosophy and Literature*, 12 (1988), 155–158.

L. R. Hirshman, "Bronte, Bloom, and Bork: An Essay on the Moral Education of Judges," *University of Pennsylvania Law Review*, 137 (1988), 177–231.

L. Keita, "'Theory Incommensurability' and Kuhn's History of Science: A Critical Analysis," *Diogenes*, 143 (1988), 41–65.

A. J. M. Garrett, "Probability, Philosophy and Science: A Briefing for Bayesians," in *Maximum Entropy and Bayesian Methods*, ed. J. Skilling (Dordrecht: Kluwer, 1989), 107–116.

D. N. McCloskey, "Why I Am No Longer a Positivist," *Review of Social Economy*, 47 (1989), 225–238.

K. E. Stanovich, review of *The Psychology of Reading* by K. Rayner and A. Pollatsek, *Journal of Reading Behavior*, 21 (1989), 425–429.

H. Wautischer, "A Philosophical Inquiry to Include Trance in Epistemology," *Journal of Psychoactive Drugs*, 21 (1989), 35–46.

Bibliography

S. D. Hunt, "Truth in Marketing Theory and Research," *Journal of Marketing*, 54 (1990), 1–15.

K. Jodkowski, "Wspolnoty uczonych, paradygmaty i rewolucje naukowe," in *Realizm, Racjonalnosc, Relatywizm*, vol. 22 (Lublin: MCS Publishing House, 1990), 439–452.

J. H. Nichols and C. Wright, *From Political Economy to Economics – and Back?* (Richmond, Calif.: ICS Press, 1990), 230.

K. E. Stanovich, "A Call for an End to the Paradigm Wars in Reading Research," *Journal of Reading Behavior*, 22 (1990), 221–231.

A. J. Underwood, "Experiments in Ecology and Management: Their Logics, Functions and Interpretations," *Australian Journal of Ecology*, 15 (1990), 365–389.

C. Beed, "Philosophy of Science and Contemporary Economics: An Overview," *Journal of Post-Keynesian Economics*, 13 (1991), 459–494.

S. D. Hunt, "Positivism and Paradigm Dominance in Consumer Research: Toward Critical Pluralism and Rapprochement," *Journal of Consumer Research*, 18 (1991), 32–44.

A. D. Irvine, "Thought Experiments in Scientific Reasoning," in *Thought Experiments in Science and Philosophy*, ed. T. Horowitz and G. J. Massey (Savage, Md.: Rowman & Littlefield, 1991), 149–165.

K. Jodkowski, "Zdemaskowanie bandy czterech (irracjonalistow)," in *Realizm, Racjonalnosc, Relatywizm*, vol. 7 (Lublin: MCS Publishing House, 1991), 109–131.

F. Merrell, "Thought Signs: Jungle or Wasteland?" *Kodikas Code: Ars Semeiotica*, 14 (1991), 215–236.

F. Selleri and A. Vandermerwe, "Karl Popper at Ninety: Highlights of a Lifelong Intellectual Quest," *Foundations of Physics*, 21 (1991), 1375–1386.

A. W. Sparkes, *Talking Philosophy* (London and New York: Routledge, 1991), 113, 124, 288.

Bibliography

K. E. Stanovich, "Cognitive Science Meets Beginning Reading," *Psychological Science*, 2 (1991), 70, 77–81.

S. Yates, "Stove o neutralizowaniu slow wskazujacych na sukces," transl. K. Jodkowski, in *Realizm, Racjonalnosc, Relatywizm*, vol. 7 (Lublin: MCS Publishing House, 1991), 165–173.

R. Brown, "Contemporary Work (1980–1988)," in *Essays on Philosophy in Australia*, ed. J. T. J. Srzednicki and D. Wood (Dordrecht, Boston, London: Kluwer, 1992), 282–284.

J. Gerrand, "Philosophy I" (letter), *The Skeptic* (Australia), 12:4 (Summer 1992), 50–51.

B. Maund, "History and Philosophy of Science in Australia," in *Essays on Philosophy in Australia*, ed. J. T. J. Srzednicki and D. Wood (Dordrecht, Boston, London: Kluwer, 1992), 242, 247.

A. L. Panchen, *Classification, Evolution, and the Nature of Biology* (Cambridge: Cambridge University Press, 1992), 308.

J. Snowden, and W. Grey, "Philosophy II" (letters), *The Skeptic* (Australia), 12:4 (Summer 1992), 51.

B. Gandy, "Popper: A Defence," *The Skeptic* (Australia), 13:2 (Winter 1993), 47–48.

G. M. MacDonald, "Methodological Falsification and the Interpretation of Paleoecological Records: The Cause of the Early Holocene Birch Decline in Western Canada," *Review of Palaeobotany and Palynology*, 79 (1993), 83–97.

N. Maxwell, "Induction and Scientific Realism: Einstein versus Van Fraassen," *British Journal for the Philosophy of Science*, 44 (1993), 61–79.

A. Musgrave, "Popper on Induction," *Philosophy of the Social Sciences*, 23 (1993), 516–527.

J. Snowden, "Popper Questioned" (letter), *The Skeptic* (Australia), 13:3 (Spring 1993), 53.

Bibliography

D. Miller, *Critical Rationalism* (Chicago: Open Court, 1994), 52–54.

K. Windschuttle, "History as a Social Science: Relativism, Hermeneutics and Induction," chap. 7 in *The Killing of History* (Sydney: Macleay Press, 1994), 185–226; and (San Francisco: Encounter Books, 1996), 203–205.

J. Agassi, "The Theory and Practice of Critical *Ratio*nalism," in *The Problem of Rationality in Science and Its Philosophy*, ed. J. Misiek (Dordrecht: Kluwer, 1995), 6.

J. Coulter, "Conceptual Transformations," *Sociological Theory*, 13 (1995), 163–177.

J. Bricmont, "Science of Chaos or Chaos in Science?" in *The Flight from Science and Reason*, ed. P. R. Gross, N. Levitt, and M. W. Lewis, Annals of the New York Academy of Sciences, 775 (New York, 1996), 168.

S. Haack, "Towards a Sober Sociology of Science," in *The Flight from Science and Reason*, ed. P. R. Gross, N. Levitt, and M. W. Lewis, Annals of the New York Academy of Sciences, 775 (New York, 1996), 259, 264.

R. Corvi, *An Introduction to the Thought of Karl Popper* (London and New York: Routledge, 1997), 168.

R. Kimball, "Who Was David Stove?" *New Criterion*, 15:7 (March 1997), 21–28; rev. and repr. in D. C. Stove, *Against the Idols of the Age* (New Brunswick, N.J., and London: Transaction Publishers, 1999), vii–xxxii; and in R. Kimball, *Lives of the Mind: The Use and Abuse of Intelligence from Hegel to Wodehouse* (Chicago: Ivan R. Dee, 2002), 246–273; discussed in L. Congdon, "Essays Gathered to Celebrate, Lament Modern Intellectual Rigors," *Washington Times*, October 6, 2002, B8; N. Malcolm, "What Tradition Has Done for Us," *Sunday Telegraph* (London), December 29, 2002, 14; and P. Coleman, "The Genius of Nonsense," *Weekend Australian*, March 29, 2003, B24.

Bibliography

J. Michell, "Quantitative Science and the Definition of Measurement in Psychology," *British Journal of Psychology*, 88 (1997), 355–383.

O. Postel-Vinay, "Relativism Feeds the Irrational Trend" (interview of J. Bricmont), *La Recherche*, 298 (May 1997), 82–85.

A. Sokal and J. Bricmont, *Impostures intellectuelles* (Paris: Éditions Odile Jacob, 1997), 61, 63, 71, 270; transl. as *Intellectual Impostures* (London: Profile, 1998), 59, 60, 67, 270; and as *Fashionable Nonsense* (New York: Picador, 1998), 61, 63, 71, 294.

J. Franklin, "Two Cultures At It Again," *Quadrant*, 42:12 (December 1998), 75–76.

S. C. Hetherington, "Stove's New Irrationalism," *Australasian Journal of Philosophy*, 76 (1998), 244–249.

C. Hood, *The Art of the State: Culture, Rhetoric, and Public Management* (Oxford: Oxford University Press, 1998), 171.

R. Kimball, *Tenured Radicals* (Chicago: Ivan R. Dee, 1998), 50.

M. Lynch, "The Discursive Production of Uncertainty: The O. J. Simpson 'Dream Team' and the Sociology of Knowledge Machine," *Social Studies of Science*, 28 (1998), 829–868.

P. P. McGuinness, "The Art of Playing a 'Straight Bat'," *Sydney Morning Herald*, December 19, 1998, 30.

K. Windschuttle, "Science, Nonsense and David Stove" (preprint of the Foreword to D. C. Stove, *Anything Goes*), *Quadrant*, 42:12 (December 1998), 10–16.

R. Champion, "Popper Proponent Pots Back," *The Skeptic* (Australia), 19:3 (Spring 1999), 40–41.

A. Olding, "Popper for Afters," *Quadrant*, 43:12 (December 1999), 19–22.

K. Windschuttle, "Civil Society and the Academic Left," *Quadrant*, 43:7–8 (July/August 1999), 25–29.

Bibliography

M. Ferrero Melgar, "Quantum Physics and Objectivity," *Arbor: Ciencia, Pensamiento y Cultura*, 167 (2000), 459–473.

A. Flew, "Against the New Irrationalism," *New Zealand Rationalist and Humanist*, Spring 2000, online at www.nzarh.org.nz/journal/spring00.htm

J. Franklin, "Last Bastion of Reason," *New Criterion*, 18:9 (May 2000), 76–77.

N. Koertge, "'New Age' Philosophies of Science: Constructivism, Feminism and Postmodernism," *British Journal for the Philosophy of Science*, 51 Supp. (2000), 667–683.

L. Trevanion, "Sub-Stove v. Sub-Chalmers" (letter), *The Skeptic* (Australia), 20:2 (Winter 2000), 8; discussed in S. Campbell, "Philosophy of Science" (letter), *The Skeptic* (Australia), 20:3 (Spring 2000), 65.

J. Franklin, "Resurrecting Logical Probability," *Erkenntnis*, 55 (2001), 277–305.

J. Franklin, *The Science of Conjecture* (Baltimore and London: Johns Hopkins University Press, 2001), 385, 406; discussed in S. Campbell, review of *The Science of Conjecture* by J. Franklin, *Interdisciplinary Science Reviews*, 27 (2002), 158–160.

M. Gardner, "A Skeptical Look at Karl Popper," *Skeptical Inquirer*, 25:4 (2001), 13–14, 72; and online at www.stephenjaygould.org/ctrl/gardner_popper.html#see

F. J. Hibberd, "Gergen's Social Constructionism, Logical Positivism and the Continuity of Error – Part 1: Conventionalism," *Theory and Psychology*, 11 (2001), 297–321.

P. Lança, "The Perils of Showmanship," *Salisbury Review*, 19:4 (Summer 2001), 36–39; discussed in J. Franklin and R. Kimball, letters, *Salisbury Review*, 20:1 (Autumn 2001), 41.

N. M. L. Nathan, *The Price of Doubt* (London: Routledge, 2001), 8.

Bibliography

D. Sredl, "Response to 'The Idea of Nursing Science' by S. D. Edwards (1999)," *Journal of Advanced Nursing*, 35 (2001), 386–387.

R. Champion, "Patroller of the Stratosphere of Ideas," *Quadrant*, 46:5 (May 2002), 39–43.

T. Jiang, "A Buddhist Scheme for Engaging Modern Science: The Case of Taixu," *Journal of Chinese Philosophy*, 29 (2002), 550.

A. E. McGrath, *A Scientific Theology*, vol. 2, *Reality* (Edinburgh: T&T Clark, 2002), 62.

J. Agassi, *Science and Culture* (Dordrecht: Kluwer, 2003), 40.

J. Franklin, "Philosophy, A Matter of Life and Death," *The Australian*, December 8, 2003, 9.

J. Franklin, *Corrupting the Youth* (Sydney: Macleay Press, 2003), 316–318, 441.

David Papineau, "Comments on Gerd Gigerenzer," in *Observation and Experiment in the Natural and Social Sciences*, ed. M. C. Galavotti (Dordrecht: Kluwer, 2003), 142.

P. Munz, Beyond *Wittgenstein's Poker: New Light on Popper and Wittgenstein* (Aldershot, UK: Ashgate, 2004), 205.

J. A. Passmore, "Contemporary Concepts of Philosophy," in *Philosophical Problems Today*, vol. 2, *Language, Meaning, Interpretation*, ed. G. Fløistad (Dordrecht: Kluwer, 2004), 23.

D. C. Anderson, *Decadence: The Passing of Personal Virtue and Its Replacement by Political and Psychological Slogans* (London: Social Affairs Unit, 2005), 238.

F. A. Murphy, *God Is Not a Story: Realism Revisited* (Oxford: Oxford University Press, 2007), 92.

J. Agassi, *A Philosopher's Apprentice* (Amsterdam and New York: Editions Rodopi, 2008), 241–242.

Bibliography

R. C. Brown, *Are Science and Mathematics Socially Constructed? A Mathematician Encounters Postmodern Interpretations of Science* (Singapore: World Scientific Publishing Co., 2009), 37.

J. Franklin, *What Science Knows: And How It Knows It* (New York and London: Encounter Books, 2009), 16, 27–29, 38–39, 138–139.

The Rationality of Induction.
Oxford: Clarendon Press, 1986.

Bibliography

REVIEWS

D. Papineau, "Stemming the Tide," *Times Literary Supplement*, 4367 (December 19, 1986), 1429.

G. Botterill, in *Philosophical Books*, 28 (1987), 189–192.

M. B. Brown, in *History and Philosophy of Logic*, 8 (1987), 116–120.

M. Giaquinto, in *Philosophy of Science*, 54 (1987), 612–615.

A. D. Irvine, in *Canadian Philosophical Reviews*, 7 (1987), 464–466.

D. Baird, in *Review of Metaphysics*, 42 (1988), 411–413.

A. D. Cling, in *Modern Schoolman*, 65 (1988), 292–294.

N. Griffin, in *Dialogue* (Canada), 27 (1988), 178–181.

D. Miller, in *Philosophy*, 63 (1988), 286–288.

H. E. Kyburg Jr., in *Noûs*, 23 (1989), 396–399.

L. Baccari, in *Aquinas*, 33 (1990), 453–455.

J. Hawthorn, in *International Studies in Philosophy*, 22:1 (1990), 137–138.

X. Verley, in *Revue Philosophique de la France et de l'étranger*, 115 (1990), 716–719.

DISCUSSION AND CITATION

C. Belshaw, "Scepticism and Madness," *Australasian Journal of Philosophy*, 67 (1989), 447–451.

B. Gower, "Stove on Inductive Scepticism," *Australasian Journal of Philosophy*, 68 (1990), 109–112.

B. Indurkhya, "Some Remarks on the Rationality of Induction," *Synthese*, 85 (1990), 95–114.

D. M. Armstrong, "What Makes Induction Rational?" *Dialogue* (Canada), 30 (1991), 503–511.

Bibliography

J. Franklin, "Healthy Skepticism," *Philosophy*, 66 (1991), 305–324.

D. M. Frankford, "Privatizing Health-Care: Economic Magic to Cure Legal Medicine," *Southern California Law Review*, 66 (1992), 1–98.

R. Brown, "Contemporary Work (1980–1988)," in *Essays on Philosophy in Australia*, ed. J. T. J. Srzednicki and D. Wood (Dordrecht, Boston, London: Kluwer, 1992), 284–286.

A. D. Irvine, "Gaps, Gluts and Paradox," in *Return of the A Priori*, ed. P. Hanson and B. Hunter, *Canadian Journal of Philosophy* Supplementary vol. 18 (Calgary: University of Calgary Press, 1992), 273–299.

R. O'Donnell, "Keynes's Weight of Argument and Popper's Paradox of Ideal Evidence," *Philosophy of Science*, 59 (1992), 44–52.

M. E. Brady, "J. M. Keynes's Theoretical Approach to Decision-Making under Conditions of Risk and Uncertainty," *British Journal for the Philosophy of Science*, 44 (1993), 357–376.

M. Rowan, "Stove on the Rationality of Induction and the Uniformity Thesis," *British Journal for the Philosophy of Science*, 44 (1993), 561–566.

J. P. Zappen, "The Logic and Rhetoric of John Stuart Mill," *Philosophy and Rhetoric*, 26 (1993), 191–200.

J. Maratos, "Ideology in Science Education: The Australian Example," *International Review of Education*, 41 (1995), 357–369.

P. Maher, "The Hole in the Ground of Induction," *Australasian Journal of Philosophy*, 74 (1996), 423–432.

C. Norris, "New Idols of the Cave, Ontological Relativity, Anti-Realism, and Interpretation Theory," *Southern Humanities Review*, 30 (1996), 209–245.

A. G. Padgett, "The Mutuality of Theology and Science: An Example from Time and Thermodynamics," *Christian Scholar's*

Bibliography

Review, 26 (1996), 12–35; and online at www2.luthersem.edu/apadgett/mutuality.html

S. C. Hetherington, "Stove's New Irrationalism," *Australasian Journal of Philosophy*, 76 (1998), 244–249.

R. R. Soberano, "Disarming Stove's Paradox: In Defence of Formal Logic," *The Paideia Project* (Twentieth World Congress of Philosophy, 1998), online at www.bu.edu/wcp/Papers/Logi/LogiSobe.htm

J. Fox, "Deductivism Surpassed," *Australasian Journal of Philosophy*, 77 (1999), 447–464.

S. Campbell, "The Fallacy of Inductive Skepticism," *The Skeptic* (Australia), 21:1 (Autumn 2001), 25–30; discussed in T. Train, "Philosophy, *&*%$ Philosophy"; L. Trevanion, "Skepticism about Induction"; S. Campbell, "Response to Tim Train"; and S. Campbell, "Response to Lawrence Trevanion," all in *The Skeptic* (Australia), 21:2 (Winter 2001), 62–66.

S. Campbell, "Fixing a Hole in the Ground of Induction," *Australasian Journal of Philosophy*, 79 (2001), 553–563.

J. Franklin, "Resurrecting Logical Probability," *Erkenntnis*, 55 (2001), 277–305.

S. Hetherington, "Why There Need Not Be Any Grue Problem about Inductive Inference as Such," *Philosophy*, 76 (2001), 127–136.

M. Huemer, "The Problem of Defeasible Justification," *Erkenntnis*, 54 (2001), 375–397.

T. McGrew, "Direct Inference and the Problem of Induction," *Monist*, 84 (2001), 153–178.

T. Edis, *The Ghost in the Universe* (Amherst, N.Y.: Prometheus Books, 2002), 273.

D. Murdoch, "Induction, Hume, and Probability," *Journal of Philosophy*, 99 (2002), 185–199.

Bibliography

J. Franklin, *Corrupting the Youth* (Sydney: Macleay Press, 2003), 338–339.

D. J. Hyder, "Kantina Metaphysics and Hertzian Mechanics," in *The Vienna Circle and Logical Empiricism*, ed. F. Stadler (Dordrecht: Kluwer, 2003), 33.

S. Campbell and J. Franklin, "Randomness and the Justification of Induction," *Synthese*, 138 (2004), 79–99.

J. Franklin, *What Science Knows: And How It Knows It* (New York and London: Encounter Books, 2009), 13.

J. Vickers, "The Problem of Induction," *The Stanford Encyclopedia of Philosophy*, Spring 2010, online at plato.stanford.edu/archives/spr2010/entries/induction-problem

---

The Plato Cult and Other Philosophical Follies.
Oxford: Basil Blackwell, 1991.

CONTENTS

Acknowledgements

Preface

Index

Bibliography

TRANSLATION

El Culto de Platón y Otras Locaras Filosóficas. Translated by Eugenia Martín. Madrid: Ediciones Catedra SA, 1993.

REVIEWS

S. Blackburn, "The Ways of Going Wrong," *Times Literary Supplement*, 4586 (February 22, 1991), 21.

P. Coleman, "Minority of One?" *News Weekly*, June 8, 1991, 21.

H. O. Mounce, in *Philosophical Investigations*, 14 (1991), 351–356.

E. Bencivenga, "Non e' per i filosofi lo spirito di patata," *Il Sole-24 Ore* (Italy), January 19, 1992, 24.

J.-L. Brandl, in *Kriterion*, 2:3 (1992), 42–47.

G. D., "Book Notes," *Ethics*, 102 (1992), 701–702.

A. Flew, in *Philosophical Books*, 33 (1992), 25–27.

J. Largeault, in *Revue Philosophique de la France et de l'étranger*, 117 (1992), 572–575.

J. J. C. Smart, in *Australasian Journal of Philosophy*, 70 (1992), 123–126.

J. J. MacIntosh, "The Plato Cult and Other Philosophical Follies," *Victorian Review*, 19 (1993), 81–85.

A. O'Hear, in *Philosophical Quarterly*, 43 (1993), 264–266.

D. D. Todd, in *Dialogue* (Canada), 32 (1993), 402–405.

A. D. Irvine, in Canadian *Philosophical Reviews*, 14 (1994), 59–63.

DISCUSSION AND CITATION

M. Devitt, "Aberrations of the Realism Debate," *Philosophical Studies*, 61 (1991), 43–63.

J. Barham, "From Enzymes to E = mc^2: A Reply to Critics," *Journal of Social and Evolutionary Systems*, 15 (1992), 249–306.

Bibliography

J. Largeault, "Émile Meyerson, philosophe oublié," *Revue Philosophique de la France et de l'étranger*, 117 (1992), 273–295.

K. Mulligan, "Post-Continental Philosophy: Nosological Notes," *Stanford French Review*, 16 (1992), 133.

R. A. Sorensen, *Pseudo-Problems: How Analytic Philosophy Gets Done* (London: Routledge, 1993), 291.

W. G. Lycan, "Conditional Reasoning and Conditional Logic," *Philosophical Studies*, 76 (1994), 223–245.

R. Nola, "There Are More Things in Heaven and Earth, Horatio, Than Are Dreamt of in Your Philosophy: A Dialogue on Realism and Constructivism," *Studies in History and Philosophy of Science*, 25 (1994), 689–727.

P. Simons, "Austrian Tradition in German Philosophy and Its Importance for Central and Eastern Europe," *Voprosy Filosofii*, 5 (1994), 64–74.

P. Slezak, "The Social Construction of Social Constructionism," *Inquiry*, 37 (1994), 139–157.

K. Windschuttle, "History as a Social Science: Relativism, Hermeneutics and Induction," chap. 7 in *The Killing of History* (Sydney: Macleay Press, 1994), 185–226, and (San Francisco: Encounter Books, 1996), 203–250.

J. J. MacIntosh, "Teaching Philosophy," *The Oxford Companion to Philosophy*, ed. T. Honderich (Oxford: Oxford University Press, 1995), 867–868.

J. Maratos, "Ideology in Science Education: The Australian Example," *International Review of Education*, 41 (1995), 357–369.

C. Cheyne and C. R. Pigden, "Pythagorean Powers or a Challenge to Platonism," *Australasian Journal of Philosophy*, 74 (1996), 639–645.

P. R. Gross, "Introduction," in *The Flight from Science and Reason*, ed. P. R. Gross, N. Levitt, and M. W. Lewis, Annals of the New York Academy of Sciences, 775 (New York, 1996), 7.

Bibliography

S. Haack, "Preposterism and Its Consequences," *Social Philosophy and Policy*, 13:2 (1996), 296–315.

S. Haack, "Reflections on Relativism: From Momentous Tautology to Seductive Contradiction," *Noûs*, 30 (1996), 297–315.

S. Haack, "Towards a Sober Sociology of Science," in *The Flight from Science and Reason*, ed. P. R. Gross, N. Levitt, and M. W. Lewis, Annals of the New York Academy of Sciences, 775 (New York, 1996), 259, 264.

A. Musgrave, "Realism, Truth and Objectivity," in *Realism and Anti-Realism in the Philosophy of Science*, ed. R. S. Cohen, R. Hilpinen, and Q. Renzong (Dordrecht: Kluwer, 1996), 40.

C. L. Brace, "The Intellectual Standing of Charles Darwin, and the Legacy of the 'Scottish Enlightenment' in Biological Thought," *Yearbook of Physical Anthropology*, 40 (1997), 91–111.

R. Kimball, "Who Was David Stove?" *New Criterion*, 15:7 (March 1997), 21–28; rev. and repr. in D. C. Stove, *Against the Idols of the Age* (New Brunswick, N.J., and London: Transaction Publishers, 1999), vii–xxxii; and in R. Kimball, *Lives of the Mind: The Use and Abuse of Intelligence from Hegel to Wodehouse* (Chicago: Ivan R. Dee, 2002), 246–273; discussed in L. Congdon, "Essays Gathered to Celebrate, Lament Modern Intellectual Rigors," *Washington Times*, October 6, 2002, B8; N. Malcolm, "What Tradition Has Done for Us," *Sunday Telegraph* (London), December 29, 2002, 14; and P. Coleman, "The Genius of Nonsense," *Weekend Australian*, March 29, 2003, B24.

R. O. Andreasen, "A New Perspective on the Race Debate," *British Journal for the Philosophy of Science*, 49 (1998), 199–225.

S. Haack, *Manifesto of a Passionate Moderate* (Chicago and London: University of Chicago Press, 1998), 147.

R. Kimball, *Tenured Radicals* (Chicago: Ivan R. Dee, 1998), 50, 187–188.

Bibliography

M. R. Matthews, "The Nature of Science and Science Teaching," *International Handbook of Science Education*, Part 2 (Dordrecht: Kluwer, 1998), 993.

A. Musgrave, "Putnams modell-theoretisches Argument gegen den Realismus," in *Kritischer Rationalismus und Pragmatismus*, ed. V. Gadenne (Amsterdam: Editions Rodopi, 1998), 181–201.

P. Slezak, "Sociology of Scientific Knowledge and Science Education," in *Constructivism in Science Education: A Philosophical Examination*, ed. M. R. Matthews (Dordrecht: Kluwer, 1998), 162.

L. Stubenberg, *Consciousness and Qualia* (Amsterdam: John Benjamins Publishing Co., 1998), 314.

A. Musgrave, "Conceptual Idealism and Stove's Gem," in *Language, Quantum, Music*, ed. M. L. Dalla Chiara, R. Giuntini, and F. Laudisa, Synthese Library, vol. 281 (Dordrecht: Kluwer, 1999), 25–35; repr. in A. Musgrave, *Essays on Realism and Rationalism* (Amsterdam: Editions Rodopi, 1999), 177–184; and as "Idealism and Antirealism," in *Scientific Inquiry: Readings in the Philosophy of Science*, ed. R. Klee (New York: Oxford University Press, 1999), 344–352.

R. O. Andreasen, "Race: Biological Reality or Social Construct?" *Philosophy of Science*, 67 Supp. (2000), S653–S666.

D. Hedley, *Coleridge, Philosophy and Religion: Aids to Reflection and the Mirror of the Spirit* (Cambridge: Cambridge University Press, 2000), 298.

R. Kimball, "The Difficulty of Hegel," *New Criterion*, 19:1 (September 2000), 4.

M. R. Matthews, *Time for Science Education* (New York: Kluwer, 2000), 324.

P. Simons, "The Four Phases of Philosophy: Brentano's Theory and Austria's History," *Monist*, 83 (2000), 68–88.

Bibliography

P. Slezak, "A Critique of Radical Social Constructivism," in *Constructivism in Education*, ed. D. C. Phillips (Chicago: National Society for the Study of Education, 2000), 92.

F. Kroon, "The Semantics of 'things in themselves': A Deflationary Account," *Philosophical Quarterly*, 51 (2001), 165–181.

B. Smith, "Fiat Objects," *Topoi*, 20 (2001), 131–148.

M. Stenmark, *Scientism: Science, Ethics and Religion* (Aldershot, UK: Ashgate, 2001), 48.

W. Sweet, *Idealism, Metaphysics, and Community* (Aldershot, UK: Ashgate, 2001), 21, 25, 26.

Louis Groarke, *The Good Rebel: Understanding Freedom and Morality* (Cranbury, N.J.: Associated University Presses, 2002), 106.

R. Kimball, "George Santayana," *New Criterion*, 20:6 (February 2002), 19.

J. Franklin, *Corrupting the Youth* (Sydney: Macleay Press, 2003), 114–115, 125, 311, 322, 331, 377–379, 388, 440, 441.

P. Barlow, *Time Present and Time Past* (Aldershot, UK: Ashgate, 2005), 194.

S. Blackburn, *Truth: A Guide for the Perplexed* (New York: Oxford University Press, 2005), 47.

A. Gottlieb, "The Truth Wars," *New York Times Book Review*, July 24, 2005, 20.

O. Benson, and J. Stangroom, *Why Truth Matters* (London and New York: Continuum, 2006), 31.

G. Englebretsen, *Bare Facts and Naked Truths* (Aldershot, UK: Ashgate, 2006), 142.

D. Clegg, "Our Food Choices Deserve Ethical Examination," *Spokesman-Review* (Spokane, Wash.), October 27, 2007, 3 E.

S. Jacobs, *The Wrong House* (Rotterdam: 010 Publishers, 2007), 129.

Bibliography

D. McDermid, "Metaphysics," in *Columbia Companion to Twentieth-Century Philosophies*, ed. Constantin V. Boundas (New York: Columbia University Press, 2007), 164.

W. G. Lycan, *Philosophy of Language: A Contemporary Introduction*, 2nd ed. (New York: Routledge, 2008), 196.

G. Harman, *Prince of Networks: Bruno Latour and Metaphysics* (Melbourne: re.press, 2009), 177.

J. Franklin, *What Science Knows: And How It Knows It* (New York and London: Encounter Books, 2009), 46–47.

El Culto de Platón y Otras Locaras Filosóficas.
  Translated by Eugenia Martín. Madrid: Ediciones Catedra SA, 1993.
See *The Plato Cult and Other Philosophical Follies* (1991)

Cricket versus Republicanism and Other Essays.
  Edited by James Franklin and R. J. Stove, with a Preface by Peter Coleman. Sydney: Quakers Hill Press, 1995.

  CONTENTS
  Acknowledgements
  Preface: Not of Our Time, *by Peter Coleman*
  Introduction, *by James Franklin*
  A Note on Editing
    1. Cricket versus Republicanism
    2. A Hero Not of Our Time
    3. A Farewell to Arts: Marxism, Semiotics and Feminism
    4. Helps to Young Authors
    5. The Intellectual Capacity of Women

Bibliography

REVIEWS

C. Ledsham, "A Farewell to Philosophy," *The Horatian*, Summer 1994–1995, 41–45.

R. Fox, in *Australasian Journal of Philosophy*, 73 (1995), 511.

J. Griffin, "'Sunny' Writer's Dry Essays Fail to Whip up Storm," *The Australian*, May 3, 1995, 12.

K. Jacka, "A Child of the Enlightenment," *Salisbury Review*, 14:2 (December 1995), 41–42.

P. P. McGuinness, "Not Simply Cricket," *Sydney Morning Herald*, January 6, 1995, 10; discussed in F. Jackson, "Man Smart, Woman Smarter? A Dead-Heat" (letter), *Sydney Morning Herald*, January 11, 1995, 12; R. Manne, "Dismayed by Praise for a Racist and a Crank," *Melbourne Age*, January 11, 1995, 11; and P. Coleman, "Facts Ignored by Pious Manne" (letter), *Melbourne Age*, January 13, 1995, 10.

B. Medlin, "Formidable Mind at Work," *Adelaide Review*, 134 (January 1995), 27–28.

Bibliography

M. Sheehan, in *Policy*, 11:1 (Autumn 1995), 50–51.

T. Stephens, "No Flies on the Barmy Army," *Sydney Morning Herald*, January 7, 1995, 18.

DISCUSSION AND CITATION

Anon., "Booknotes," *Philosophy*, 70 (1995), 299–300.

Anon., "A 'Corrosive' Freethinker," *Uniken* (University of New South Wales), February 17, 1995, 12.

Anon., "'Politically Correct' Attack on Stove," *Heraclitus*, 40 (March 1995), 14.

B. Faust, "Unthrifty Writers," *Australian Rationalist*, 38 (1995), 38–42.

A. Field, "Expect No Mercy from a Fearless Questioner," *Courier Mail*, March 1, 1995, 8.

J. R. Flynn, "Group Differences: Is the Good Society Impossible?" *Journal of Biosocial Science*, 28 (1996), 573–585.

R. Kimball, "Who Was David Stove?" *New Criterion*, 15:7 (March 1997), 21–28; rev. and repr. in D. C. Stove, *Against the Idols of the Age* (New Brunswick, N.J., and London: Transaction Publishers, 1999), vii–xxxii; and in R. Kimball, *Lives of the Mind: The Use and Abuse of Intelligence from Hegel to Wodehouse* (Chicago: Ivan R. Dee, 2002), 246–273; discussed in L. Congdon, "Essays Gathered to Celebrate, Lament Modern Intellectual Rigors," *Washington Times*, October 6, 2002, B8; N. Malcolm, "What Tradition Has Done for Us," *Sunday Telegraph* (London), December 29, 2002, 14; and P. Coleman, "The Genius of Nonsense," *Weekend Australian*, March 29, 2003, B24.

K. Green, "A Plague on Both Your Houses," *Monist*, 82 (1999), 278–303.

J. W. Tuttleton, *The Primate's Dream* (Chicago: Ivan R. Dee, 1999), 299.

Bibliography

J. R. Flynn, *How to Defend Humane Ideals: Substitutes for Objectivity* (n.p.: University of Nebraska Press, 2000), 145.

J. Franklin, "Thomas Kuhn's Irrationalism," *New Criterion*, 18:10 (June 2000), 29–34.

J. Franklin, "Stove's Discovery of the Worst Argument in the World," *Philosophy*, 77 (2002), 615–624; and online at www.maths.unsw.edu.au/~jim/worst.pdf; discussed in B. Smith, "Beyond Concepts," in *Formal Ontology in Information Systems: Proceedings of the Third International Conference*, ed. A. C. Varsi and L. Vieu (Amsterdam: IOS Press, 2004), 74.

J. Franklin, *Corrupting the Youth* (Sydney: Macleay Press, 2003), 127, 441.

R. Kimball, *The Rape of the Masters: How Political Correctness Sabotages Art* (New York: Encounter Books, 2004), 16.

C. Abel and T. Fuller, *The Intellectual Legacy of Michael Oakeshott* (Exeter, UK: Imprint Academic, 2005), 241.

F. J. Hibberd, *Unfolding Social Constructionism* (New York: Springer Science, 2005), 172.

M. Engel, "A Simple Matter of Difference," *Financial Times* (London), December 9, 2006, 2.

J. McDonald, "It's Still the Sweetest Victory of All," *The Age* (Melbourne), December 19, 2006, 13.

J. McDonald, "No Sympathy as Nation Savours Joy of Cricket," *Sydney Morning Herald*, December 19, 2006, 11.

J. Warhurst, "Republicanism Is Just Not on the Ball," *Canberra Times*, January 18, 2007.

M. Engel, "High Balls and Low Shots," *Observer* (London), July 5, 2009.

R. Kimball, "Speaking Up for the Fifties," *New Criterion*, 26:10 (June 2008), 2.

Bibliography

J. Franklin, *What Science Knows: And How It Knows It* (New York and London: Encounter Books, 2009), 46, 246.

Darwinian Fairytales.

Edited by James Franklin. Aldershot, UK: Avebury / Ashgate Publishing, 1995.

CONTENTS

Acknowledgements

Preface

TRANSLATION

"Bajki darwinowskie," *Problemy Genezy*, 16 (2008), 25–36, 37–56, and passim.

REVISED EDITION

Darwinian Fairytales: Selfish Genes, Errors of Heredity, and Other Fables of Evolution. With an Introduction by Roger Kimball. New York: Encounter Books, 2006.

Bibliography

REVIEWS

M. Fitzgerald, "Dawkins Son of Darwin Meets His Match," *Perspective*, December 1996, 13–15.

A. Olding, in *Australasian Journal of Philosophy*, 75 (1997), 133–135; repr. in *Rationalist News* (Journal of the Rationalist Association of New South Wales), 31:2 (April 1997), 8–9.

M. T. Ghiselin, in *History and Philosophy of the Life Sciences*, 20 (1998), 108–110.

D. Fontana, in *Scientific and Medical Network*, 68 (December 1998), 45–48.

J. C. McCarthy, "The Descent of Science," *Review of Metaphysics*, 52 (1999), 835–866.

D. Palmer, "The Agnostic Who Took on Darwin and Dawkins," *News Weekly*, March 7, 2009, 12–14.

DISCUSSION AND CITATION

S. Blackburn, "I Rather Think I Am a Darwinian," *Philosophy*, 71 (1996), 605–616.

J. Franklin, "Stove's Anti-Darwinism," *Philosophy*, 72 (1997), 133–136.

R. Kimball, "Who Was David Stove?" *New Criterion*, 15:7 (March 1997), 21–28; rev. and repr. in D. C. Stove, *Against the Idols of the Age* (New Brunswick, N.J., and London: Transaction Publishers, 1999), vii–xxxii; and in R. Kimball, *Lives of the Mind: The Use and Abuse of Intelligence from Hegel to Wodehouse* (Chicago: Ivan R. Dee, 2002), 246–273; discussed in L. Congdon, "Essays Gathered to Celebrate, Lament Modern Intellectual Rigors," *Washington Times*, October 6, 2002, B8; N. Malcolm, "What Tradition Has Done for Us," *Sunday Telegraph* (London), December 29, 2002, 14; and P. Coleman, "The Genius of Nonsense," *Weekend Australian*, March 29, 2003, B24.

Bibliography

J. O'Sullivan, "On Being a Rootless Cosmopolitan," *National Review*, 49:24 (December 22, 1997), 6.

R. Kimball, *Tenured Radicals* (Chicago: Ivan R. Dee, 1998), 50, 188.

R. J. Neuhaus, "The Public Square," *First Things*, 80 (February 1998), 62–78.

R. Kimball, "Preface," in W. Bagehot, *Physics and Politics, or, Thoughts on the Application of the Principles of "Natural Selection" and "Inheritance" to Political Society* (Chicago: Ivan R. Dee, 1999), xxvii.

J. C. McCarthy, "The Descent of Science," *Review of Metaphysics*, 52 (1999), 835–866.

S. R. L. Clark, *Biology and Christian Ethics* (Cambridge: Cambridge University Press, 2000), 64.

W. Grey, "Metaphor and Meaning," *Minerva: An Internet Journal of Philosophy*, 4 (November 2000), online at www.ul.ie/~philos/vol4/metaphor.html

J. Teichman, "Dr. Jekyll & Mr. Hyde," *New Criterion*, 19:2 (October 2000), 65.

P. Lança, "The Perils of Showmanship," *Salisbury Review*, 19:4 (Summer 2001), 36–39; discussed in J. Franklin and R. Kimball, letters, *Salisbury Review*, 20:1 (Autumn 2001), 41.

J. Franklin, *Corrupting the Youth* (Sydney: Macleay Press, 2003), 333.

A. Gibson, *Metaphysics and Transcendence* (London: Routledge, 2003), 6.

J. Teichman, "Darwinism," *Quadrant*, 47:3 (March 2003), 36–37.

R. Kimball, *The Rape of the Masters: How Political Correctness Sabotages Art* (New York: Encounter Books, 2004), 168.

J. Teichman, "Darwin, Malthus and Professor Jones," *Think: Philosophy for Everyone*, 7 (Summer 2004), 91–94.

Bibliography

P. Dizikes, "Science Chronicle," *New York Times Book Review*, June 11, 2006, 28.

J. Rosenblum, "Mommy, Why Are Atheists Dim-Witted?" *Jerusalem Post*, December 15, 2006, 15.

K. Behrens, "Kindness to a Stranger," *Daily Times-Call* (Longmont, Col.), April 2, 2008, A4.

D. Berlinski, *The Devil's Delusion: Atheism and Its Scientific Pretensions* (New York: Crown / Random House, 2008), 165.

M. Novak, *No One Sees God: The Dark Night of Atheists and Believers* (New York: Doubleday, 2008), 170.

Popper y Después.
Translated by Susana Nuccetelli. Madrid: Tecnos, 1995.
See *Popper and After: Four Modern Irrationalists* (1982)

Anything Goes: Origins of the Cult of Scientific Irrationalism.
With a Foreword by Keith Windschuttle and an Afterword by James Franklin. Paddington, NSW: Macleay Press, 1998.
See *Popper and After: Four Modern Irrationalists* (1982)

Against the Idols of the Age.
Edited with an Introduction by Roger Kimball.
New Brunswick, N.J., and London:
Transaction Publishers, 1999.

CONTENTS
Introduction: Who Was David Stove? *by Roger Kimball*
Acknowledgements and a Note on the Text

Bibliography

REVIEWS

S. Sailer, "The Unexpected Uselessness of Philosophy," *National Post* (Canada), December 28, 1999, A18; and online at www.isteve.com/Philosophy.htm

Anon., "Booknotes," *Philosophy*, 75 (2000), 313–316.

Anon., "Notes on Current Books," *Virginia Quarterly Review*, 76:3 (Summer 2000), 103.

S. Campbell, "Defending Common Sense," *Partisan Review*, 67:3 (Summer 2000), 500–503; and online at www.bu.edu/partisanreview/archive/2000/3/campbell.html; discussed in P. Coleman, "Against the Idols of the Age," *Adelaide Review*, 205 (October 2000), 6; repr. as "Notebook: The Greatest 20th-

Bibliography

Century Philosopher a Conservative Australian?" *Australian Financial Review*, October 6, 2000, 82.

S. Campbell, "Wit and Wisdom," *The Australian's Review of Books*, 5:10 (November 2000), 12–13, 26; discussed in Max Deutscher, "Think for Yourself" (letter), *The Australian's Review of Books*, 5:11 (December 2000), 4; Joe Goozeff, "Minds Collide" (letter), *The Australian's Review of Books*, 5:11 (December 2000), 4; Mick Earls, "Let Postmodernism Be" (letter), *The Australian's Review of Books*, 6:1 (February 2001), 4; and Alan McCallum, "Quote Marks Spell Success" (letter), *The Australian's Review of Books*, 6:1 (February 2001), 4; and with Campbell's reply in "By the Way" (letter), *The Australian's Review of Books*, 6:2 (March 2001), 4.

J. Derbyshire, "Philosopher's Stove: An Unexpected Pleasure," *National Review Online*, December 22, 2000–January 1, 2001, online at www.nationalreview.com/weekend/books/books-derbyshire122200.shtml

S. Goode, "Essays from an Australian Philosopher and Wit," *Washington Times*, February 27, 2000, B7.

D. Gordon, "Sweet Rationality," *Mises Review*, 6:2 (Summer 2000), 20–24; and online at mises.org/misesreview_detail.aspx?control=159

W. V. Harris, in *Philosophy and Literature*, 24 (2000), 497–499.

T. S. Hibbs, "Heat and Light: David Stove's Rage against Bad Thinking," *Weekly Standard*, 6:2 (September 18, 2000), 27–29.

A. O'Hear, "Swimming against the Tide," *Spectator*, January 29, 2000, 47–48.

S. Campbell, in *Review of Metaphysics*, 54 (2001), 943–945.

S. Tridgell, "String of Pearls," *Quadrant*, 45:1–2 (January/February 2001), 114–116; and online at www.maths.unsw.edu.au/~jim/tridgellrev.html

A. D. Irvine, in *Philosophical Books*, 43 (2002), 39–41.

Bibliography

S. Casterson, "Building Your Library – Scepticism," *Sunday Age* (Melbourne), January 29, 2006, 17.

DISCUSSION AND CITATION

P. Coleman, "Against the Idols of the Age," *Adelaide Review*, 205 (October 2000), 6; repr. as "Notebook: The Greatest 20th-Century Philosopher a Conservative Australian?" *Australian Financial Review*, October 6, 2000, 82.

P. Lança, "The Perils of Showmanship," *Salisbury Review*, 19:4 (Summer 2001), 36–39; discussed in J. Franklin and R. Kimball, letters, *Salisbury Review*, 20:1 (Autumn 2001), 41.

R. E. Ewin, *Reasons and the Fear of Death* (Lanham, Md.: Rowman & Littlefield, 2002), 80.

J. Franklin, *Corrupting the Youth* (Sydney: Macleay Press, 2003), 118, 311, 441.

Scientific Irrationalism: Origins of a Postmodern Cult.
  With a Foreword by Keith Windschuttle and an Afterword by James Franklin. New Brunswick, N.J., and London: Transaction Publishers, 2001.

See *Popper and After: Four Modern Irrationalists* (1982)

On Enlightenment.
  Edited with an Introduction by Andrew Irvine
  and a Preface by Roger Kimball. New Brunswick, N.J.,
  and London: Transaction Publishers, 2003.

CONTENTS
Preface, *by Roger Kimball*
Introduction: David Stove on Enlightenment, *by Andrew Irvine*

Bibliography

REVIEWS

J. Franklin, in *Sophia*, 42 (2003), 135–136.

M. Teichmann, in *News Weekly*, April 5, 2003, 23.

J. J. C. Smart, in *Australasian Journal of Philosophy*, 81 (2003), 429–433.

J. Foss, in *Dialogue* (Canada), 44:1 (2005), 194–196.

G. Hunter, "On Enlightenment," *University of Toronto Quarterly*, 74 (Winter 2004/2005), 425–426.

D. Todd, in *Philosophy in Review*, 24 (2004), 63–68.

Bibliography

DISCUSSION AND CITATION

R. Kimball, "The Death of Socialism?" *New Criterion*, 20:8 (April 2002), 19.

A. Badiou and R. Brassier, *Saint Paul: The Foundation of Universalism* (Stanford: Stanford University Press, 2003), 63.

J. Franklin, *Corrupting the Youth* (Sydney: Macleay Press, 2003), 441.

D. C. Anderson, *Decadence: The Passing of Personal Virtue and Its Replacement by Political and Psychological Slogans* (London: Social Affairs Unit, 2005), 238.

R. Kimball, "Gallimaufry & More: On the new *Oxford Dictionary of National Biography*," *New Criterion*, 23:5 (January 2005), 10.

R. Kimball, "On Liberty, or, How John Stuart Mill Went Wrong," in *Civic Education and Culture*, ed. B. C. S. Watson (Wilmington, Del.: ISI Books, 2005), pp. 31, 33.

J. Jordan, *Pascal's Wager* (Oxford: Oxford University Press, 2006), 192.

R. Kimball, "Introduction: Saving Remnants," *New Criterion*, 26:5 (January 2008), 7.

J. Foss, *Beyond Environmentalism: A Philosophy of Nature* (Hoboken, N.J.: John Wiley & Sons, 2009), 78.

What's Wrong with Benevolence: Happiness, Private Property, and the Limits of Enlightenment.
Edited with an Introduction by Andrew Irvine and a Foreword by Roger Kimball. New York, London: Encounter Books, 2011.

CONTENTS

Bibliography

B. ARTICLES

1949

"Goths Within the Gates," *Honi Soit* (Sydney University), 21:5 (April 7, 1949), 5, 8.

1950

"Liberals, Democracy and the Anti-Communist Bill," *Honi Soit* (Sydney University), 22:8 (May 4, 1950), 5.

DISCUSSION AND CITATION

P. Coleman, "Nothing but the Bill," *Honi Soit* (Sydney University), 22:10 (May 18, 1950), 4–5.

A. Barcan, *Radical Students: The Old Left at Sydney University* (Melbourne: Melbourne University Press, 2002), 247.

J. Franklin, *Corrupting the Youth* (Sydney: Macleay Press, 2003), 158.

1952

Critical Notice of *The Conditions of Knowing* by A. Sinclair, *Australasian Journal of Philosophy*, 30 (1952), 47–61.

"A Note on 'Relativism'," *Australasian Journal of Philosophy*, 30 (1952), 188–191.

1955

"Two Problems about Individuality," *Australasian Journal of Philosophy*, 33 (1955), 183–188.

DISCUSSION AND CITATION

J. Bobik, "A Note on a Problem about Individuality," *Australasian Journal of Philosophy*, 36 (1958), 210–215.

J. Franklin, *Corrupting the Youth* (Sydney: Macleay Press, 2003), 355.

Bibliography

1958

"Are Professors Overpaid?" *Observer* (Australia), April 19, 1958, 133–134.

1959

"Popperian Confirmation and the Paradox of the Ravens," *Australasian Journal of Philosophy*, 37 (1959), 149–151.

DISCUSSION AND CITATION

J. W. N. Watkins, "Mr Stove's Blunders," *Australasian Journal of Philosophy*, 37 (1959), 240–241; with Stove's reply in "A Reply to Mr Watkins" (1960).

J. L. Mackie, "The Paradox of Confirmation," *British Journal for the Philosophy of Science*, 13 (1963), 265–277.

1960

Critical Notice of *The Logic of Scientific Discovery* by K. Popper, *Australasian Journal of Philosophy*, 38 (1960), 173–187.

DISCUSSION AND CITATION

J. Agassi, "The Role of Corroboration in Popper's Methodology," *Australasian Journal of Philosophy*, 39 (1961), 82–91.

"A Reply to Mr Watkins" [commentary on J. W. N. Watkins, "Mr Stove's Blunders," *Australasian Journal of Philosophy*, 37 (1959), 240–241], *Australasian Journal of Philosophy*, 38 (1960), 51–54.

DISCUSSION AND CITATION

W. J. Huggett, "Discussion: On Not Being Gulled by Ravens," *Australasian Journal of Philosophy*, 38 (1960), 48–50.

J. W. N. Watkins, "Reply to Mr Stove's Reply," *Australasian Journal of Philosophy*, 38 (1960), 54–58.

P. C. Gibbons, "On the Severity of Tests," *Australasian Journal of Philosophy*, 40 (1962), 79–82.

Bibliography

J. L. Mackie, "The Paradox of Confirmation," *British Journal for the Philosophy of Science*, 13 (1963), 265–277.

"Two Cultures? or Goodbye to All That," *Australian Highway* (Workers' Educational Association of NSW), 41:3 (June 1960), 57–60.

DISCUSSION AND CITATION

E. Kalmar, K. Moon, S. Tick, and T. H. Jones, "Heat over Stove" (letters), *Australian Highway* (Workers' Educational Association of NSW), 41:4 (September 1960), 90–93.

1962

"John Anderson and Cultural Freedom in Australia," *Free Spirit* (Australian Association for Cultural Freedom), 8:1 (May/June 1962), 6–7.

DISCUSSION AND CITATION

A. Barcan, *Radical Students: The Old Left at Sydney University* (Melbourne: Melbourne University Press, 2002), 247, 270, 320, 377.

J. Franklin, *Corrupting the Youth* (Sydney: Macleay Press, 2003), 41–42.

1964

"Velikovsky in Collision," *Quadrant*, 8:4 (October/November 1964), 35–44.

REPRINTED

Kronos, 6:3 (April 1981), 18–33.

DISCUSSION AND CITATION

R. E. Juergens, "Aftermath to Exposure," in *The Velikovsky Affair*, ed. A. de Grazia (New York: University Books, and London: Sidgwick & Jackson, 1966), 50–79; and rev., ed. A. de Grazia, R. E. Juergens, and L. C. Stecchini (London: Sphere Books, 1978), 54–79.

Bibliography

C. L. Ellenberger, "Focus: A Point of View," *SIS Review* (Society for Interdisciplinary Studies), 3:2 (1978), 29.

C. L. Ellenberger, "Documents: Heretics, Dogmatists and Science's Reception of New Ideas," *Kronos*, 4:4 (June 1979), 67.

H. H. Bauer, *Beyond Velikovsky* (Champaign, Ill.: University of Illinois Press, 1999), 54, 56–57, 79, 213, 263.

1965

"Hempel and Goodman on the Ravens," *Australasian Journal of Philosophy*, 43 (1965), 300–310.

"Hume, Probability, and Induction," *Philosophical Review*, 74 (1965), 160–177.

REPRINTED

Bobbs-Merrill Reprint Series in Philosophy, no. PHL 203, n.d., 160–177.

Hume, ed. V. C. Chappell (Garden City, N.Y.: Anchor Books / Doubleday, 1966), 187–212; repr. as *Hume: A Collection of Critical Essays* (Notre Dame: University of Notre Dame Press; London and Melbourne: Macmillan, 1968), 187–212.

Philosophy Today, no. 3, ed. J. H. Gill (London: Macmillan, 1970), 212–232.

David Hume: Critical Assessments, vol. 2, *Induction, Scepticism*, ed. S. Tweyman (London and New York: Routledge, 1995), 29–43.

DISCUSSION AND CITATION

D. Goldstick, "Hume's 'Circularity' Charge against Inductive Reasoning," *Dialogue* (Canada), 11 (1972), 258–266.

B. Stroud, "Causality and the Inference from the Observed to the Unobserved: The Negative Phase," chap. 3 in *Hume* (London: Routledge & Kegan Paul, 1977), 42–67.

Bibliography

W. E. Morris, "Hume's Refutation of Inductive Probabilism," in *Probability and Causality*, ed. J. H. Fetzer (Dordrecht: Reidel, 1988), 43–77.

H. Thomas, "Modal Realism and Inductive Skepticism," *Noûs*, 27 (1993), 331–354.

P. J. R. Millican, "Hume's Argument Concerning Induction: Structure and Interpretation," in *David Hume: Critical Assessments*, vol. 2, *Induction, Scepticism*, ed. S. Tweyman (London and New York: Routledge, 1995), 91–144; repr. in *Hume: General Philosophy*, ed. D. W. D. Owen (Aldershot, UK: Ashgate, 2000), 165–218.

S. Tweyman, "Introduction," in *David Hume: Critical Assessments*, vol. 2: *Induction, Scepticism*, ed. S. Tweyman (London and New York: Routledge, 1995), xix.

R. Lantin, "Hume and the Problem of Induction," *Philosophia*, 26:1–2 (1998), 105–117.

T. McGrew, "Direct Inference and the Problem of Induction," *Monist*, 84 (2001), 153–178.

1966

"Hempel's Paradox," *Dialogue* (Canada), 4 (1966), 444–455.

"On Logical Definitions of Confirmation," *British Journal for the Philosophy of Science*, 16 (1966), 265–272.

"Out of Their Own Mouths" (short extract from Stove's "The Revolution at Berkeley," unpublished), *Broadsheet* (Sydney Libertarian Society), 50 (November 1966), 6; discussed by Stove in "Letters to the Editors" (a letter explaining how the extract gives a misleading impression of Stove's views), *Broadsheet* (Sydney Libertarian Society), 51 (May 1967), 9.

Bibliography

1967

"Keynes, John Maynard," in *The Encyclopedia of Philosophy*, ed.
P. Edwards (New York: Free Press, and London: Macmillan, 1967),
vol. 4, 333–334.

(With C. A. Hooker), "Relevance and the Ravens," *British Journal
for the Philosophy of Science*, 18 (1967), 305–315.

DISCUSSION AND CITATION

L. Gibson, "On 'Ravens and Relevance' and a Likelihood
Solution of the Paradox of Confirmation," *British Journal for the
Philosophy of Science*, 20 (1969), 75–80.

J. L. Mackie, "The Relevance Criterion of Confirmation,"
British Journal for the Philosophy of Science, 20 (1969), 27–40.

C. A. Hooker, "The Ravens, Hempel and Goodman,"
Australasian Journal of Philosophy, 49 (1971), 82–89.

B. Maund, "History and Philosophy of Science in Australia," in
Essays on Philosophy in Australia, ed. J. T. J. Srzednicki and D.
Wood (Dordrecht, Boston, London: Kluwer, 1992), 251.

"The Scientific Mafia: The Velikovsky Story," *Honi Soit* (Sydney
University), 40:20 (September 7, 1967), 10–11.

REPRINTED

As "The Scientific Mafia," *Science Yearbook* (Sydney: Sydney
University Science Association, 1969), 96–101.

As "The Scientific Mafia," *Pensée*, 2 (May 1972), 6–7.

As "The Scientific Mafia," in *Velikovsky Reconsidered*, by the
Editors of *Pensée* (Garden City, N.Y.: Doubleday, 1976), 5–12.

As "The Velikovsky Story: The Scientific Mafia," online at
www.saturniancosmology.org/files/velikovsky/scimafia.txt

DISCUSSION AND CITATION

H. H. Bauer, *Beyond Velikovsky* (Champaign, Ill.: University of
Illinois, 1999), 79.

"University Letter: The Humphreys Affair," *Quadrant*, 11:3 (May/June 1967), 54–56.

DISCUSSION AND CITATION

J. Franklin, *Corrupting the Youth* (Sydney: Macleay Press, 2003), 289.

1970

"Deductivism," *Australasian Journal of Philosophy*, 48 (1970), 76–98.

DISCUSSION AND CITATION

F. N. Harpley, "Hume's Probabilism," *Australasian Journal of Philosophy*, 49 (1971), 146–151.

J. Hearne, "Deductivism and Practical Reasoning," *Philosophical Studies*, 45 (1984), 205–208.

T. Govier, "What Is a Good Argument?" *Metaphilosophy*, 23 (1992), 393–409.

J. Franklin, *Corrupting the Youth* (Sydney: Macleay Press, 2003), 338.

E. Brandon, "Philosophy as Bricolage," in *What Philosophy Is*, ed. H. Carel and D. Gamez (London and New York: Continuum, 2004), 134.

"Mr Gibson on Ravens and Relevance," *British Journal for the Philosophy of Science*, 21 (1970), 287–288.

"Santamaria and the Philosophers," *Honi Soit* (Sydney University), 43:32 (October 29, 1970), 6, 11.

DISCUSSION AND CITATION

J. Franklin, *Corrupting the Youth* (Sydney: Macleay Press, 2003), 291–292.

"University Notes: Sydney," *Quadrant*, 14:2 (March/April 1970), 37–39.

Bibliography

DISCUSSION AND CITATION

J. Franklin, *Corrupting the Youth* (Sydney: Macleay Press, 2003), 289.

1972

"Misconditionalisation," *Australasian Journal of Philosophy*, 50 (1972), 173–183.

DISCUSSION AND CITATION

P. Tichy, *The Foundations of Frege's Logic* (Berlin: Walter de Gruyter, 1988), 118.

B. Brown, "Defending Backwards Causation," *Canadian Journal of Philosophy*, 22 (1992), 429–443.

J. Woods, A. Irvine, and D. Walton, *Argument: Critical Thinking, Logic and the Fallacies* (Toronto: Prentice Hall Canada, 2000), 157; 2nd ed. (2004), 163.

G. Oddie, *Value, Reality, and Desire* (Oxford: Oxford University Press, 2005), 66.

1973

"An Error in Selby-Bigge's Hume," *Australasian Journal of Philosophy*, 51 (1973), 77.

"Laws and Singular Propositions," *Australasian Journal of Philosophy*, 51 (1973), 139–143.

1975

"Dr Johnson, British Moralist," *Quadrant*, 19:4 (July 1975), 83–86.

REPRINTED

As "British Moralists," in *Quadrant: Twenty-Five Years*, ed. P. Coleman, L. Shrubb, and V. Smith (St. Lucia: University of Queensland Press, 1982), 380–387.

"Hume, the Causal Principle and Kemp Smith," *Hume Studies*, 1 (1975), 1–24.

Bibliography

DISCUSSION AND CITATION

E. Craig, "Hume's Letter to Stewart," *Hume Studies*, 1 (1975), 70–75.

F. E. Sparshott, "In Defense of Kemp Smith," *Hume Studies*, 1 (1975), 66–69.

H. B. Dalrymple, "Hume's Causal Principle," *Southwest Philosophical Studies*, 1 (1976), 46–49.

R. J. Glossop, "In Defence of David Hume," *Australasian Journal of Philosophy*, 55 (1977), 59–63.

T. Penelhum, "Hume's Skepticism and the *Dialogues*," in *McGill Hume Studies*, ed. D. Norton, D. Capaldi, and W. L. Robison (San Diego: Austin Hill Press, 1979), 253–278.

1976

"David Hume: 1776–1976," *Quadrant*, 20:11 (November 1976), 52–54.

"Hume, Induction and the Irish" [commentary on S. Blackburn, "Past Certainties and Future Possibilities" (review of Probability and Hume's Inductive Scepticism by D. C. Stove), *Times Literary Supplement*, 3727 (August 10, 1973), 935; I. Hinckfuss, review of *Probability and Hume's Inductive Scepticism* by D. C. Stove, *Australasian Journal of Philosophy*, 52 (1974), 269–276; and J. E. Adler, "Stove on Hume's Inductive Scepticism," *Australasian Journal of Philosophy*, 53 (1975), 167–170], *Australasian Journal of Philosophy*, 54 (1976), 140–147.

DISCUSSION AND CITATION

M. C. Bradley, "Stove on Hume," *Australasian Journal of Philosophy*, 55 (1977), 69–73.

I. Hinckfuss, "Stove, Induction and the Irish," *Australasian Journal of Philosophy*, 55 (1977), 64–68.

C. Mortensen, "Koopman, Stove and Hume," *Australasian Journal of Philosophy*, 55 (1977), 74–75.

Bibliography

G. J. D. Moyal, and S. Tweyman, *Early Modern Philosophy: Metaphysics, Epistemology, and Politics – Essays in Honour of Robert F. McRae* (Delmar, N.Y.: Caravan Books, 1986), 134.

"Why Should Probability Be the Guide of Life?" in *Hume: A Re-Evaluation*, ed. D. W. Livingston and D. T. King (New York: Fordham University Press, 1976), 50–68.

REPRINTED

What? Where? When? Why? Essays on Induction, Space, Time, Explanation, ed. R. McLaughlin (Dordrecht and Boston: Reidel, 1982), 27–48.

DISCUSSION AND CITATION

D. W. Livingston and D. T. King, "Introduction," in *Hume: A Re-Evaluation* (New York: Fordham University Press, 1976), 7–8.

R. McLaughlin, "Preface," in *What? Where? When? Why: Essays on Induction, Space, Time, Explanation* (Dordrecht and Boston: Reidel, 1982), xv.

W. Salmon, "Further Reflections," in *What? Where? When? Why? Essays on Induction, Space, Time, Explanation* (Dordrecht and Boston: Reidel, 1982), 239–245.

1977

"The Force of Intellect: Fifty Years of John Anderson," *Quadrant*, 21:7 (July 1977), 45–46.

DISCUSSION AND CITATION

S. A. Grave, *A History of Philosophy in Australia* (St. Lucia: University of Queensland Press, 1984), 47, 69.

J. Franklin, *Corrupting the Youth* (Sydney: Macleay Press, 2003), 42, 48–49.

R. Jeffery, "An Early Influence: John Anderson," in *Remembering Hedley*, ed. M. Thatcher and C. Bell (Canberra: Australian National University Press, 2008), 25.

Bibliography

"Hume, Kemp Smith and Carnap," *Australasian Journal of Philosophy*, 53 (1977), 189–200.

1978

"On Hume's Is-Ought Thesis," *Hume Studies*, 4 (1978), 64–72.

DISCUSSION AND CITATION

F. Snare, *The Nature of Moral Thinking* (London and New York: Routledge, 1992), 89.

"Part IX of Hume's *Dialogue*s," *Philosophical Quarterly*, 28 (1978), 300–309.

REPRINTED

David Hume: Critical Assessments, vol. 5, *Religion*, ed. S. Tweyman (London and New York: Routledge, 1995), 254–264.

DISCUSSION AND CITATION

J. Franklin, "More on Part IX of Hume's *Dialogue*s," *Philosophical Quarterly*, 30 (1980), 69–71; repr. in *David Hume: Critical Assessments*, vol. 5, *Religion*, ed. S. Tweyman (London and New York: Routledge, 1995), 278–281.

D. Livingston, "Philosophy of History and Philosophy of Religion," in N. Capaldi, J. King, and D. Livingston, "The Hume Literature of the 1970s," *Philosophical Topics*, 12 (1981), 182–192.

B. Calvert, "Another Problem about Part IX of Hume's *Dialogue*s," *International Journal for Philosophy of Religion*, 14 (1983), 65–70; repr. in *David Hume: Critical Assessments*, vol. 5, *Religion*, ed. S. Tweyman (London and New York: Routledge, 1995), 286–291.

D. E. Stahl, "Hume's *Dialogue* IX Defended," *Philosophical Quarterly*, 34 (1984), 505–507.

J. Dye, "A Word on Behalf of Demea," *Hume Studies*, 15

(1989), 120–140; repr. in *David Hume: Critical Assessments*, vol. 5, *Religion*, ed. S. Tweyman (London and New York: Routledge, 1995), 265–277; and rev. and repr. in "Victor and Vanquished in Part IX" (1998), online at www.niu.edu/~jdye/Victor.html

E. Scribano, "The *A priori* Proof of the Existence of God in 18th-Century England: From Cudworth to Hume," *Giornale critico della filosofia italiana*, 9 (1989), 184–212.

E. J. Khamara, "Hume versus Clarke on the Cosmological Argument," *Philosophical Quarterly*, 42 (1992), 34–55.

J. K. Campbell, "Hume's Refutation of the Cosmological Argument," *International Journal for Philosophy of Religion*, 40 (1996), 159–173.

"The Plurality of Worlds: A *Dialogue*," *Proceedings of the Russellian Society* (Sydney University), 3 (1978), 37–64.

REPRINTED

In part in *Quadrant*, 23:1–2 (January/February 1979), 37–41.

"Popper on Scientific Statements," *Philosophy*, 53 (1978), 81–88.

DISCUSSION AND CITATION

M. Rowan and A. Smithson, "Stove on Popper's Scientific Statements," *Philosophy*, 55 (1980), 258–262.

D. R. Oldroyd, *The Arch of Knowledge: An Introductory Study of the History of the Philosophy and Methodology of Science* (New York: Methuen, 1986), 314.

"The Problem of Induction," *Proceedings of the Russellian Society* (Sydney University), 3 (1978), 11–23.

DISCUSSION AND CITATION

A. W. Sparkes, *Talking Philosophy* (London and New York: Routledge, 1991), 125, 126, 288.

Bibliography

1979

"The Nature of Hume's Skepticism," in *McGill Hume Studies*, ed. D. F. Norton, N. Capaldi, and W. L. Robison (San Diego: Austin Hill Press, 1979), 203–225.

REPRINTED

David Hume: Critical Assessments, vol. 2, *Induction, Scepticism*, ed. S. Tweyman (London and New York: Routledge, 1995), 274–294.

DISCUSSION AND CITATION

N. Capaldi, "The Problem of Hume and Hume's Problem," in *McGill Hume Studies*, ed. D. F. Norton, N. Capaldi, and W. L. Robison (San Diego: Austin Hill Press, 1979), 3–21.

G. J. D. Moyal and S. Tweyman, *Early Modern Philosophy: Metaphysics, Epistemology, and Politics – Essays in Honour of Robert F. McRae* (Delmar, N.Y.: Caravan Books, 1986), 124, 134.

T. W. Tilley, "Hume on God and Evil: Dialogues X and XI as Dramatic Conversation," *Journal of the American Academy of Religion*, 56 (1988), 703–726.

1982

"British Moralists." See "Dr Johnson, British Moralist" (1975).

"How Popper's Philosophy Began," *Philosophy*, 57 (1982), 381–387.

DISCUSSION AND CITATION

J. M. Brown, "Popper Had a Brand New Bag," *Philosophy*, 59 (1984), 512–515.

1983

"Hume's Argument about the Unobserved," in *Studies in the Eighteenth Century*, vol. 5, ed. J. P. Hardy and J. C. Eade (Oxford: The Voltaire Foundation / Taylor Institution, 1983), 189–206.

Bibliography

"Velikovsky Become Respectable," *Quadrant*, 27:10 (October 1983), 75–76.

REPRINTED

As "Velikovsky and the Cosmic Serpent: Velikovsky Become Respectable," *Kronos*, 9:3 (June 1984), 40–44.

DISCUSSION AND CITATION

S. V. M. Clube and W. M. Napier, "Velikovskians in Collision," *Quadrant*, 28:1–2 (January/February 1984), 33–34; repr. in *Kronos*, 9:3 (June 1984), 44–48; with Stove's reply in "D. C. Stove: A Rejoinder" (1984).

1984

"D. C. Stove: A Rejoinder" [commentary on S. V. M. Clube and W. M. Napier, "Velikovskians in Collision," *Quadrant*, 28:1–2 (January/February 1984), 33–34], *Quadrant*, 28:1–2 (January/February 1984), 35.

REPRINTED

Kronos, 9:3 (June 1984), 49–50.

"The Feminists and the Universities," *Quadrant*, 28:9 (September 1984), 8.

DISCUSSION AND CITATION

P. Coleman, *Commonwealth of Australia Parliamentary Debates (Hansard): House of Representatives*, 139, 11 September 1984, 1048; discussed in R. A. Crowley, *Commonwealth of Australia Parliamentary Debates (Hansard): Senate*, S.105, 12 September 1984, 886; S. M. Ryan, *Commonwealth of Australia Parliamentary Debates (Hansard): Senate*, S.105, 12 September 1984, 886–887; and P. Coleman, *Commonwealth of Australia Parliamentary Debates (Hansard): House of Representatives*, 139, 13 September 1984, 1317; all also online (with occasional minor differences in pagination) at search.aph.gov.au/search

179

Bibliography

H. Trinca, "Professor 'Flunks,' in Feminist Row," *The Australian*, September 7, 1984, 3; with Stove's reply in "Universities and Feminists Once More" (1984).

M. Lawrence, "New Attack on Uni 'Jobs for the Girls'," *Sydney Morning Herald*, April 11, 1986, 2.

F. C. L. Allen, "Indicators of Academic Excellence: Is There a Link between Merit and Reward?" *Australian Journal of Education*, 34 (1990), 87–98.

J. Franklin, "The Sydney Philosophy Disturbances," *Quadrant*, 43:4 (April 1999), 16–21; and online at www.maths.unsw.edu.au/~jim/sydq.html

J. Franklin, *Corrupting the Youth* (Sydney: Macleay Press, 2003), 308.

"Paralytic Epistemology, or the Soundless Scream" [commentary on P. Feyerabend, "On the Limits of Research," *New Ideas in Psychology*, 2 (1984), 3–7], *New Ideas in Psychology*, 2 (1984), 21–24.

REPRINTED

D. C. Stove, *Cricket versus Republicanism and Other Essays* (Sydney: Quakers Hill Press, 1995), 49–54.

D. C. Stove, *Against the Idols of the Age* (New Brunswick, N.J., and London: Transaction Publishers, 1999), 71–77.

D. C. Stove, *On Enlightenment* (New Brunswick, N.J., and London: Transaction Publishers, 2002), 141–146.

DISCUSSION AND CITATION

R. Kimball, "'Openness' & 'The Closing of the American Mind'," *New Criterion*, 26:3 (November 2007), 17.

"Universities and Feminists Once More" [commentary on H. Trinca, "Professor 'Flunks,' in Feminist Row," *The Australian*, September 7, 1984, 3], *Quadrant*, 28:11 (November 1984), 60–61.

Bibliography

DISCUSSION AND CITATION

M. Lawrence, "New Attack on Uni 'Jobs for the Girls'," *Sydney Morning Herald*, April 11, 1986, 2.

J. Franklin, *Corrupting the Youth* (Sydney: Macleay Press, 2003), 308.

"Velikovsky and the Cosmic Serpent: Velikovsky Become Respectable." See "Velikovsky Become Respectable" (1983).

1985

"Cole Porter and Karl Popper, or the Jazz Age in the Philosophy of Science," *Proceedings of the Russellian Society* (Sydney University), 10 (1985), 14–30.

REPRINTED

As "Karl Popper and the Jazz Age," *Encounter*, 65:1 (June 1985), 65–74.

As "Cole Porter and Karl Popper: The Jazz Age in the Philosophy of Science," in D. C. Stove, *The Plato Cult and Other Philosophical Follies* (Oxford: Basil Blackwell, 1991), 1–26.

As "Cole Porter and Karl Popper: The Jazz Age in the Philosophy of Science," in D. C. Stove, *Against the Idols of the Age* (New Brunswick, N.J., and London: Transaction Publishers, 1999), 3–32.

DISCUSSION AND CITATION

J. R. Skoyles and S. R. Wray, "Stove's Popper" (letters), *Encounter*, 65:3 (September/October 1985), 78; with Stove's reply in "Reply by D. C. Stove" (1985).

M. Hofri, "On Popper's Revaluation" (letter), together with Stove's untitled reply, *Encounter*, 65:4 (November 1985), 80.

E. Nagel, "Nagel, Popper, Stove" (letter), *Encounter*, 65:5 (December 1985), 78.

Bibliography

P. Watter, "Stove's Popper" (letter), together with Stove's untitled reply, *Encounter*, 65:5 (December 1985), 78.

W. W. Bartley III, "Facts and Fictions" (letter), together with Stove's untitled reply, *Encounter*, 66:1 (January 1986), 77–78.

G. Robinson, "Karl Popper and the Jazz Age" (letter), together with Stove's untitled reply, *Encounter*, 66:2 (February 1986), 80.

J. S. Lieberson, "Karl Popper and the Jazz Age" (letter), together with Stove's untitled reply, *Encounter*, 66:3 (March 1986), 78–79.

L. D. Gasman, "Stove's Popper" (letter), together with Stove's untitled reply, *Encounter*, 66:5 (May 1986), 77.

T. Theocharis, "Stove and Popper" (letter), *Encounter* 67:3 (September/October 1986), 79–80.

T. Hollick, "Popper and '*t2*'" (letter), *Encounter* 67:2 (July/August 1986), 80; with Stove's reply in "Stove and Popper" (1986).

G. N. Schlesinger, "Truth, Humility, and Philosophers," in *God and the Philosophers*, ed. T. V. Morris (Oxford: Oxford University Press, 1996), 258.

R. Kimball, "Little god, big Wilson," *New Criterion*, 18:6 (February 2000), 6.

C. Hayes, *Fallibilism, Democracy and the Market* (Lanham, Md.: University Press of America, 2001), 28, 33, 58, 68, 104.

R. Kimball, "The Museum as Fun House," *New Criterion*, 19:6 (February 2001), 10; rev. and repr. in R. Kimball, *Art's Prospect: The Challenge of Tradition in an Age of Celebrity* (Christchurch: Cybereditions, 2002), 13–26.

P. Coleman, "Deep Impact," *Weekend Australian*, August 31, 2002, B8.

Bibliography

K. Marra, and R. A. Schanke, *Staging Desire: Queer Readings of American Theater History* (Ann Arbor: University of Michigan Press, 2002), 163.

J. Franklin, *Corrupting the Youth* (Sydney: Macleay Press, 2003), 319.

"Jobs for the Girls: Feminist Vapours," *Quadrant*, 29:5 (May 1985), 34–35.

REPRINTED

As "Jobs for the Girls," in D. C. Stove, *On Enlightenment* (New Brunswick, N.J., and London: Transaction Publishers, 2002), 159–163.

DISCUSSION AND CITATION

L. M. Garcia, "Uni Jobs: Equality v Quality Claimed," *Sydney Morning Herald*, May 10, 1985, 3.

P. Shrubb, "Jobs for the Girls," *Quadrant*, 29:7 (July 1985), 14–16.

M. Lawrence, "New Attack on Uni 'Jobs for the Girls'," *Sydney Morning Herald*, April 11, 1986, 2.

M. Thornton, "Hegemonic Masculinity and the Academy," *International Journal of the Sociology of Law*, 17 (1989), 115–130.

P. Stavropoulos, "Conservative Intellectuals and Feminism," *Australian Journal of Political Science*, 25 (1990), 218–227.

J. Franklin, "The Sydney Philosophy Disturbances," *Quadrant*, 43:4 (April 1999), 16–21; and online at www.maths.unsw.edu.au/~jim/sydq.html

J. Franklin, *Corrupting the Youth* (Sydney: Macleay Press, 2003), 308.

"Karl Popper and the Jazz Age." See "Cole Porter and Karl Popper, or the Jazz Age in the Philosophy of Science" (1985).

"Reply by D. C. Stove" [commentary on J. R. Skoyles and S. R. Wray, "Stove's Popper" (letters), *Encounter*, 65:3 (September/October 1985), 78], *Encounter*, 65:3 (September/October 1985), 78–79.

1986

"David Stove Replies" [commentary on I. Donaldson, B. C. Birchall, B. Thorn, P. Redding, J. Burnheim, A. J. Dunston, and S. M. Jack, "A Farewell to Arts: Replies to David Stove, with His Rebuttal" (letters), *Quadrant*, 30:7–8 (July/August 1986), 9–14], *Quadrant*, 30:7–8 (July/August 1986), 14–15.

"A Farewell to Arts: Marxism, Semiotics and Feminism," *Quadrant*, 30:5 (May 1986), 8–11.

REPRINTED

D. C. Stove, *Cricket versus Republicanism and Other Essays* (Sydney: Quakers Hill Press, 1995), 14–24.
Online at www.maths.unsw.edu.au/~jim/arts.html

DISCUSSION AND CITATION

M. Lawrence, "New Attack on Uni 'Jobs for the Girls'," *Sydney Morning Herald*, April 11, 1986, 2.

I. Donaldson, B. C. Birchall, B. Thorn, P. Redding, J. Burnheim, A. J. Dunston, and S. M. Jack, "A Farewell to Arts: Replies to David Stove, with His Rebuttal" (letters), *Quadrant*, 30:7–8 (July/August 1986), 9–14; with Stove's reply in "David Stove Replies" (1986).

P. Stavropoulos, "Conservative Intellectuals and Feminism," *Australian Journal of Political Science*, 25 (1990), 218–227.

S. Haack, "Preposterism and Its Consequences," *Social Philosophy and Policy*, 13 (1996), 296–315.

R. Kimball, "Who Was David Stove?" *New Criterion*, 15:7 (March 1997), 21–28; rev. and repr. in D. C. Stove, *Against the Idols of the Age* (New Brunswick, N.J., and London: Transaction

Publishers, 1999), vii–xxxii; and in R. Kimball, *Lives of the Mind: The Use and Abuse of Intelligence from Hegel to Wodehouse* (Chicago: Ivan R. Dee, 2002), 246–273; discussed in L. Congdon, "Essays Gathered to Celebrate, Lament Modern Intellectual Rigors," *Washington Times*, October 6, 2002, B8; N. Malcolm, "What Tradition Has Done for Us," *Sunday Telegraph* (London), December 29, 2002, 14; and P. Coleman, "The Genius of Nonsense," *Weekend Australian*, March 29, 2003, B24.

J. Franklin, "The Sydney Philosophy Disturbances," *Quadrant*, 43:4 (April 1999), 16–21; and online at www.maths.unsw.edu.Ωau/~jim/sydq.html

R. Kimball, *The Long March: How the Cultural Revolution of the 1960s Changed America* (New York: Encounter Books, 2000), 47, 290.

R. Kimball, "The Perfect Academic," *National Review*, 53:20 (October 15, 2001), 56, 58.

J. Franklin, *Corrupting the Youth* (Sydney: Macleay Press, 2003), 310.

M. Devine, "More Like a Leaking Reactor Than a Liberal Arts Faculty," *Sun Herald* (Sydney), January 30, 2005, 15.

R. Kimball, "Leszek Kolakowski and the Anatomy of Totalitarianism," *New Criterion*, 23:10 (June 2005), 6.

P. Coleman, "Happy Anniversary," *The Australian*, May 4, 2006, 12.

R. Kimball, "Speaking Up for the Fifties," *New Criterion*, 26:10 (June 2008), 2.

"Stove and Popper" [commentary on T. Hollick, "Popper and '*t2*'" (letter), *Encounter*, 67:2 (July/August 1986), 80], *Encounter*, 67:3 (September/October 1986), 79.

Bibliography

1987

"The Columbus Argument," *Commentary*, 84:6 (December 1987), 57–58.

REPRINTED

As part of "Why You Should Be a Conservative," *Proceedings of the Russellian Society* (Sydney University), 13 (1988), 1–13.

D. C. Stove, *Cricket versus Republicanism and Other Essays* (Sydney: Quakers Hill Press, 1995), 58–62.

D. C. Stove, *On Enlightenment* (New Brunswick, N.J., and London: Transaction Publishers, 2002), 149–153.

DISCUSSION AND CITATION

J. Gouinlock, E. Alexander, B. M. Leiser, and L. Aronsohn, "John Stuart Mill" (letters), *Commentary*, 85:4 (April 1988), 6, 8–9; with Stove's reply in "David Stove Writes" (1988).

A. D. Irvine, "Bertrand Russell and Academic Freedom," *Russell*, 16 (1996), 5–36.

R. Kimball, "One Very Simple Principle," *New Criterion*, 17:3 (November 1998), 4–15; rev. and repr. as "James Fitzjames Stephen v. John Stuart Mill," in R. Kimball, *Experiments Against Reality* (Chicago: Ivan R. Dee, 2000), 159–188.

R. Kimball, "The Trivialization of Outrage: The Artworld at the End of the Millennium," *Quadrant*, 43:10 (October 1999); and online at www.mrbauld.com/arttrash.html#back6

"What Is Wrong with Our Thoughts? A Neo-Positivist Credo," *Proceedings of the Russellian Society* (Sydney University), 12 (1987), 1–20.

REPRINTED

D. C. Stove, *The Plato Cult and Other Philosophical Follies* (Oxford: Basil Blackwell, 1991), 179–205.

Bibliography

DISCUSSION AND CITATION

S. Haack, *Manifesto of a Passionate Moderate* (Chicago and London: University of Chicago Press, 1998), 147.

1988

"David Stove Replies" [commentary on R. Conway, "Roasting Freud with a Stove," *Quadrant*, 33:1–2 (January/February 1989), 58–59], *Quadrant*, 33:1–2 (January/February 1989), 59.

"David Stove Writes" [commentary on J. Gouinlock, E. Alexander, B. M. Leiser, and L. Aronsohn, "John Stuart Mill" (letters), *Commentary*, 85:4 (April 1988), 6, 8–9], *Commentary*, 85:4 (April 1988), 9–10.

"Freud: Business Arising out of the Minutes" [commentary on F. Crews, *Skeptical Engagements* (Oxford: Oxford University Press, 1986)], *Quadrant*, 32:9 (September 1988), 40–41.

DISCUSSION AND CITATION

R. Conway, "Roasting Freud with a Stove," *Quadrant*, 33:1–2 (January/February 1989), 58–59; with Stove's reply in "David Stove Replies" (1988).

J. Lovell, "Short Notes on Sigmund Freud," *Quadrant*, 33:1–2 (January/February 1989), 60.

R. Conway, "First Plumber of the Depths," *Weekend Australian*, December 9, 2000, R13.

J. Franklin, *Corrupting the Youth* (Sydney: Macleay Press, 2003), 209.

"A Hero Not of Our Time," *Quadrant*, 32:5 (May 1988), 40–43.

REPRINTED

D. C. Stove, *Cricket versus Republicanism and Other Essays* (Sydney: Quakers Hill Press, 1995), 4–13.

Bibliography

DISCUSSION AND CITATION

J. Franklin, *Corrupting the Youth* (Sydney: Macleay Press, 2003), 243.

"Righting Wrongs," *Commentary*, 85:1 (January 1988), 57–59.

REPRINTED

As part of "Why You Should Be a Conservative," *Proceedings of the Russellian Society* (Sydney University), 13 (1988), 1–13.

D. C. Stove, *On Enlightenment* (New Brunswick, N.J., and London: Transaction Publishers, 2002), 165–169.

"Why You Should Be a Conservative," *Proceedings of the Russellian Society* (Sydney University), 13 (1988), 1–13.

PREPRINTED

In part as "The Columbus Argument," *Commentary*, 84:6 (December 1987), 57–58.

In part as "Righting Wrongs," *Commentary*, 85:1 (January 1988), 57–59.

REPRINTED

In part as "The Columbus Argument," in D. C. Stove, *Cricket versus Republicanism and Other Essays* (Sydney: Quakers Hill Press, 1995), 58–62.

In part as "The Columbus Argument," in D. C. Stove, *On Enlightenment* (New Brunswick, N.J., and London: Transaction Publishers, 2002), 149–153.

In part as "Righting Wrongs," in D. C. Stove, *On Enlightenment* (New Brunswick, N.J., and London: Transaction Publishers, 2002), 165–169.

In part as "Why You Should Be a Conservative," in D. C. Stove, *On Enlightenment* (New Brunswick, N.J., and London: Transaction Publishers, 2002), 171–178.

Bibliography

DISCUSSION AND CITATION

R. Kimball, "Introduction: Saving Remnants," *New Criterion*, 26:5 (January 2008), 7.

1989

"Changing the World," *Salisbury Review*, 7:4 (June 1989), 48–50.

"D'Holbach's Dream: The Central Claim of the Enlightenment," *Quadrant*, 33:12 (December 1989), 28–31.

REPRINTED

D. C. Stove, *Cricket versus Republicanism and Other Essays* (Sydney: Quakers Hill Press, 1995), 68–77.

D. C. Stove, *Against the Idols of the Age* (New Brunswick, N.J., and London: Transaction Publishers, 1999), 81–91.

"The End of History?" [commentary on F. Fukuyama, "The End of History?" *National Interest*, 16 (Summer 1989), 3–18], *National Interest*, 17 (Fall 1989), 97–98.

REPRINTED

Quadrant, 33:10 (October 1989), 32–33.

D. C. Stove, *Cricket versus Republicanism and Other Essays* (Sydney: Quakers Hill Press, 1995), 55–57.

DISCUSSION AND CITATION

F. Fukuyama, "A Reply to My Critics," *National Interest*, 18 (Winter 1989), 21–28.

S. E. Bronner, *Moments of Decision: Political History and the Crises of Radicalism* (New York: Routledge, 1992), 127.

"The Oracles and Their Cessation: A Tribute to Julian Jaynes," *Encounter*, 72:4 (April 1989), 30–38.

REPRINTED

D. C. Stove, *Cricket versus Republicanism and Other Essays* (Sydney: Quakers Hill Press, 1995), 115–140.

Bibliography

DISCUSSION AND CITATION

W. Oxley, "Religion and Rationality" (letter), together with Stove's untitled reply, *Encounter*, 73:2 (July/August 1989), 79.

A. F. Bainbridge, "The Oracles" (letter), *Encounter*, 73:4 (November 1989), 78.

"Racial and Other Antagonisms," *Proceedings of the Russellian Society* (Sydney University), 14 (1989), 1–10.

REPRINTED

D. C. Stove, *Cricket versus Republicanism and Other Essays* (Sydney: Quakers Hill Press, 1995), 91–105.

D. C. Stove, *Against the Idols of the Age* (New Brunswick, N.J., and London: Transaction Publishers, 1999), 137–152.

DISCUSSION AND CITATION

P. Coleman, "Not of Our Time," in D. C. Stove, *Cricket versus Republicanism and Other Essays* (Sydney: Quakers Hill Press, 1995), ix.

P. P. McGuinness, "Not Simply Cricket" (review of *Cricket versus Republicanism and Other Essays*), *Sydney Morning Herald*, January 6, 1995, 10; discussed in F. Jackson, "Man Smart, Woman Smarter? A Dead-heat" (letter), *Sydney Morning Herald*, January 11, 1995, 12; R. Manne, "Dismayed by Praise for a Racist and a Crank," *Melbourne Age*, January 11, 1995, 11; and P. Coleman, "Facts Ignored by Pious Manne" (letter), *Melbourne Age*, January 13, 1995, 10.

P. Coleman, "*Quadrant* Takes a Mortal Blow," *Sydney Morning Herald*, November 18, 1997, 19.

P. Akerman, "Avoiding Reality Destroys the Case," *Daily Telegraph* (Sydney), July 5, 2001, 21.

P. Coleman, "The Intimations of Robert Manne," *Adelaide Review*, 214 (July 2001), 13.

R. Kimball, "Who Was David Stove?" *New Criterion*, 15:7 (March 1997), 21–28; rev. and repr. in D. C. Stove, *Against the Idols of the Age* (New Brunswick, N.J., and London: Transaction Publishers, 1999), vii–xxxii; and in R. Kimball, *Lives of the Mind: The Use and Abuse of Intelligence from Hegel to Wodehouse* (Chicago: Ivan R. Dee, 2002), 246–273; discussed in L. Congdon, "Essays Gathered to Celebrate, Lament Modern Intellectual Rigors," *Washington Times*, October 6, 2002, B8; N. Malcolm, "What Tradition Has Done for Us," *Sunday Telegraph* (London), December 29, 2002, 14; and P. Coleman, "The Genius of Nonsense," *Weekend Australian*, March 29, 2003, B24.

D. Wilson, *The Case for Classical Christian Education* (Wheaton, Ill.: Crossway Books, 2003), 45–46.

P. Coleman, "All That Swagger," *Quadrant*, 49:9 (September 2005), 82–84.

1990

"The Diabolical Place: A Secret of the Enlightenment," *Encounter*, 74:4 (May 1990), 9–15.

REPRINTED

D. C. Stove, *On Enlightenment* (New Brunswick, N.J., and London: Transaction Publishers, 2002), 93–110.

DISCUSSION AND CITATION

R. Kimball, "Gallimaufry & More: On the new *Oxford Dictionary of National Biography*," *New Criterion*, 23:5 (January 2005), 10.

"Enlightenment, Racism and Racial Prejudice," *Salisbury Review*, 8:4 (June 1990), 16–20.

"The Intellectual Capacity of Women," *Proceedings of the Russellian Society* (Sydney University), 15 (1990), 1–16.

Bibliography

REPRINTED

D. C. Stove, *Cricket versus Republicanism and Other Essays* (Sydney: Quakers Hill Press, 1995), 27–48.

D. C. Stove, *Against the Idols of the Age* (New Brunswick, N.J., and London: Transaction Publishers, 1999), 113–136.

DISCUSSION AND CITATION

P. P. McGuinness, "Not Simply Cricket" (review of D. C. Stove, *Cricket versus Republicanism and Other Essays*), *Sydney Morning Herald*, January 6, 1995, 10; discussed in F. Jackson, "Man Smart, Woman Smarter? A Dead-heat" (letter), *Sydney Morning Herald*, January 11, 1995, 12; R. Manne, "Dismayed by Praise for a Racist and a Crank," *Melbourne Age*, January 11, 1995, 11; and P. Coleman, "Facts Ignored by Pious Manne" (letter), *Melbourne Age*, January 13, 1995, 10.

R. Kimball, "Who Was David Stove?" *New Criterion*, 15:7 (March 1997), 21–28; rev. and repr. in D. C. Stove, *Against the Idols of the Age* (New Brunswick, N.J., and London: Transaction Publishers, 1999), vii–xxxii; and in R. Kimball, *Lives of the Mind: The Use and Abuse of Intelligence from Hegel to Wodehouse* (Chicago: Ivan R. Dee, 2002), 246–273; discussed in L. Congdon, "Essays Gathered to Celebrate, Lament Modern Intellectual Rigors," *Washington Times*, October 6, 2002, B8; N. Malcolm, "What Tradition Has Done for Us," *Sunday Telegraph* (London), December 29, 2002, 14; and P. Coleman, "The Genius of Nonsense," *Weekend Australian*, March 29, 2003, B24.

R. Christiansen, "Spreading Sweetness and Light," *Spectator*, January 25, 2001, 50; and online at www.spectator.co.uk/spectator/thisweek/20436/spreading-sweetness-and-light.thtml

J. Teichman, "The Intellectual Capacity of David Stove," *Philosophy*, 76 (2001), 149–157; repr. in J. Teichman, *Ethics and Reality: Collected Essays* (Aldershot, UK: Ashgate, 2001), 70–77.

R. Kimball, "A Reading List for Every Young Woman," *Women's Quarterly*, 33 (Autumn 2002), 11–12.

J. Franklin, *Corrupting the Youth* (Sydney: Macleay Press, 2003), 309, 366.

C. Norris and D. Roden, *Jacques Derrida*, vol. 2 (London: Sage Publications, 2003), 180, 199, 200.

P. Sheehan, "Today's Young Women – The New Men," *Sydney Morning Herald*, April 12, 2004, 17.

P. Coleman, "All That Swagger," *Quadrant*, 49:9 (September 2005), 82–84.

"O Pioneers! . . . ," *Encounter*, 74:5 (June 1990), 38–40.

REPRINTED

D. C. Stove, *Cricket versus Republicanism and Other Essays* (Sydney: Quakers Hill Press, 1995), 108–114.

As "Glimpses of Pioneer Life," in D. C. Stove, *On Enlightenment* (New Brunswick, N.J., and London: Transaction Publishers, 2002), 111–117.

1991

"The Demons and Dr Dawkins" [commentary on R. Dawkins, *The Selfish Gene* (New York: Oxford University Press, 1976)], *Proceedings of the Russellian Society* (Sydney University), 16 (1991), 1–25.

REPRINTED

American Scholar, 61:1 (Winter 1992), 67–78.

DISCUSSION AND CITATION

R. Pollack, W. Warner, and M. Levin, "The Demons and Dr Dawkins," together with Stove's untitled reply, *American Scholar*, 61:3 (Summer 1992), 477–480.

Bibliography

T. K. Shotwell, "An Essay on Beauty: Some Implications of Beauty in the Natural World," *Zygon*, 27 (1992), 479–490.

K. T. Gallagher, "Dawkins, Darwin, and Design," *American Catholic Philosophical Quarterly*, 67 (1993), 233–246.

1992

"A New Religion," *Philosophy*, 67 (1992), 233–240.

REPRINTED

D. C. Stove, *Darwinian Fairytales* (Aldershot, UK: Avebury / Ashgate, 1995), 171–177.

DISCUSSION AND CITATION

M. Levin, "Stove on Gene Worship," *Philosophy*, 68 (1993), 240–243.

N. S. Thompson and P. G. Derr, "On the Use of Mental Terms in Behavioral Ecology and Sociobiology," *Behavior and Philosophy*, 24 (1995), 31–37.

S. Blackburn, "I Rather Think I Am a Darwinian," *Philosophy*, 71 (1996), 605–616.

N. S. Thompson, "Shifting the Natural Selection Metaphor to the Group Level," *Behavior and Philosophy*, 28 (2000), 83–101.

H. Taylor, *Human Rights* (Edinburgh: Rutherford House, 2004), 23.

1993

"Errors of Heredity, or the Irrelevance of Darwinism to Human Life," *Proceedings of the Russellian Society* (Sydney University), 18 (1993), 25–35.

REPRINTED

As "So You Think You Are a Darwinian?" in *Philosophy*, 69 (1994), 267–277.

Bibliography

As "So You Think You Are a Darwinian?" in D. C. Stove, *Cricket versus Republicanism and Other Essays* (Sydney: Quakers Hill Press, 1995), 78–90.

D. C. Stove, *Darwinian Fairytales* (Aldershot, UK: Avebury / Ashgate, 1995), 212–225.

DISCUSSION AND CITATION

S. Blackburn, "I Rather Think I Am a Darwinian," *Philosophy*, 71 (1996), 605–616.

J. Franklin, "Stove's Anti-Darwinism," *Philosophy*, 72 (1997), 133–136.

A. O'Hear, *Beyond Evolution* (Oxford: Oxford University Press, 1997), 142–143.

"The Subjection of John Stuart Mill," *Philosophy*, 68 (1993), 5–13.

DISCUSSION AND CITATION

B. Brecher, "Why Patronize Feminists? A Reply to Stove on Mill," *Philosophy*, 68 (1993), 397–400.

F. G. Downing, "A Cynical Response to the Subjection of Women," *Philosophy*, 69 (1994), 229–230.

I. Thiel, "On Stove on Mill on Women," *Philosophy*, 69 (1994), 100–101.

K. Burgess-Jackson, "John Stuart Mill, Radical Feminist," *Social Theory and Practice*, 21 (1995), 369–396.

V. Allen, "On Liberty and Logic," in *Listening to Their Voices*, ed. M. M. Wertheimer (n.p.: University of South Carolina Press, 1997), 67.

B. Brecher, *Getting What You Want?* (London: Routledge, 1998), 176.

D. G. Brown, "Stove's Reading of Mill," *Utilitas*, 10 (1998), 122–126.

Bibliography

K. Green, "A Plague on Both Your Houses," *Monist*, 82 (1999), 278–303.

G. W. Smith, "J. S. Mill on What We Don't Know about Women," *Utilitas*, 12 (2000), 41–61.

J. Franklin, *Corrupting the Youth* (Sydney: Macleay Press, 2003), 366.

M. Chaudhury, *Bounds of Freedom: Popper, Liberty and Ecological Rationality* (Amsterdam and New York: Editions Rodopi, 2004), 55.

P. Coleman, "All That Swagger," *Quadrant*, 49:9 (September 2005), 82–84.

K. Burgess-Jackson, "John Stuart Mill, Radical Feminist," in *Mill's The Subjection of Women: Critical Essays*, ed. M. H. Morales (Lanham, Md.: Rowman & Littlefield, 2005), 96.

1994

"So You Think You Are a Darwinian?" See "Errors of Heredity, or the Irrelevance of Darwinism to Human Life" (1993).

2002

"Another Attempt to Prove that Induction Is Justified: The Law of Large Numbers," in *Epistemology: Contemporary Readings*, ed. M. Huemer (London and New York: Routledge, 2002), 352–368.

PREPRINTED

D. C. Stove, *The Rationality of Induction* (Oxford: Clarendon Press, 1986), 55–75.

DISCUSSION AND CITATION

R. Audi, "Introduction: A Narrative Survey of Classical and Contemporary Positions in Epistemology," in *Epistemology: Contemporary Readings*, ed. M. Huemer (London and New York: Routledge, 2002), 14.

M. Huemer, "Inductive Inference," in *Epistemology:*

Bibliography

Contemporary Readings, ed. M. Huemer (London and New York: Routledge, 2002), 296–297.

2003

"Living Retired," *Society*, 40 (2003), 78–80.

2008

"Bajki darwinowskie," *Problemy Genezy*, 16 (2008), 25–36, 37–56, and passim; see *Darwinian Fairytales*, ed. James Franklin (Aldershot, UK: Avebury / Ashgate, 1995).

C. REVIEWS

1955

Review of *Fact, Fiction and Forecast* by N. Goodman, *Australasian Journal of Philosophy*, 33 (1955), 128–132.

1956

Review of *Philosophical Essays* by A. J. Ayer, *Australasian Journal of Philosophy*, 34 (1956), 60–65.

DISCUSSION AND CITATION

J. Franklin, *Corrupting the Youth* (Sydney: Macleay Press, 2003), 42.

1958

Review of *Foundations of Inductive Logic* by R. Harrod, *Australasian Journal of Philosophy*, 36 (1958), 71–79.

Review of *Sovereign Reason* and *Logic without Metaphysics* by E. Nagel, *Australasian Journal of Philosophy*, 36 (1958), 151–153.

1960

"Beard-and-Sandals Dept?" review of *The Humanities in Australia* by A. G. Price, *Observer* (Australia), April 30, 1960, 26.

"Bertrand Russell: Andersonian," review of *The Wisdom of the West* by "B. Russell," *Nation*, 35 (January 16, 1960), 22–23.

DISCUSSION AND CITATION

C. Spadoni, "Who Wrote Bertrand Russell's Wisdom of the West?" *Papers of the American Bibliographical Society*, 80 (1986), 349–367.

L. Cumming, "A Remarkable Philosophical Hybrid: *The Wisdom of the West*," *Quadrant*, 33:1–2 (January/February 1989), 61–62.

Bibliography

J. Franklin, *Corrupting the Youth* (Sydney: Macleay Press, 2003), 51, 283.

1963

Review of *Hume's Philosophy of Belief* by A. Flew, *Australasian Journal of Philosophy*, 41 (1963), 427–432.

Review of *The Problem of Induction and Its Solution* by J. J. Katz, *Australasian Journal of Philosophy*, 41 (1963), 269–272.

1964

"Darwin's Grandfather," review of *Erasmus Darwin* by D. King-Hele, *Quadrant*, 8:2 (June/July 1964), 79–80.

1965

Review of *The Anatomy of Inquiry* by I. Scheffler, *Australasian Journal of Philosophy*, 43 (1965), 109–113.

1968

Review of *Choice and Chance* by B. Skyrms, *Australasian Journal of Philosophy*, 46 (1968), 189–191.

1969

Review of *The Problem of Inductive Logic* by I. Lakatos, *Australasian Journal of Philosophy*, 47 (1969), 243–248.

DISCUSSION AND CITATION

P. Baillie, "Falsifiability and Probability," *Australasian Journal of Philosophy*, 48 (1970), 99–100.

Review of *The Foundations of Scientific Inference* by W. Salmon, *Australasian Journal of Philosophy*, 47 (1969), 86–89.

1974

Review of *Reason and Prediction* by S. Blackburn, *Australasian Journal of Philosophy*, 52 (1974), 72–74.

Bibliography

1975

Review of *Readings in the Philosophy of Religion* by B. A. Brody, *Australasian Journal of Philosophy*, 53 (1975), 283–284.

1976

"Galton's Eugenics," review of *Francis Galton* by D. W. Forest, *Quadrant*, 20:3 (March 1976), 51–53.

Review of *The Emergence of Probability* by I. Hacking, *Australasian Journal of Philosophy*, 54 (1976), 180–181.

Review of *Hume* by T. Penelhum, *Dialogue* (Canada), 15 (1976), 505–509.

1977

"Cricket versus Republicanism," review of *On Top Down Under: Australia's Cricket Captains* by R. Robinson, *Quadrant*, 21 [mislabeled as 22]: 6 (June 1977), 36–37.

REPRINTED

D. C. Stove, *Cricket versus Republicanism and Other Essays* (Sydney: Quakers Hill Press, 1995), 1–3.

The Oxford Book of Australian Essays, ed. I. Salusinszky (Melbourne and New York: Oxford University Press, 1997), 169–170.

Online at www.maths.unsw.edu.au/~jim/cvr.html

DISCUSSION AND CITATION

G. Windsor, "These Tales of One City Give the Right Side of the Argument," *Sydney Morning Herald*, November 15, 1997, 11S.

P. Porter, "Down but Not Under," review of *The Oxford Book of Australian Essays*, *The Times* (London), March 19, 1998, 42.

1978

"Konrad Lorenz," review of *Konrad Lorenz* by A. Nesbitt, *Quadrant*, 22:2 (February 1978), 72–73.

Bibliography

Review of *Hume* by B. Stroud, *Australasian Journal of Philosophy*, 56 (1978), 90–92.

1979

"Bradman," review of *Sir Donald Bradman* by I. Rosenwater, *Quadrant*, 23:5 (May 1979), 70–71.

1980

"The Green World," review of *The Discovery of South America* by J. H. Parry, *Quadrant*, 24:6 (June 1980), 77–78.

"A Lovesome Thing," review of *A History of British Gardening* by M. Hadfield, *Quadrant*, 24:3 (March 1980), 78–79.

1981

"Minute Detail," review of *London and the Life of Literature in Late Victorian England: The Diary of George Gissing* by P. Coustillas, *Quadrant*, 25:4 (April 1981), 71–72.

1982

"A Question of Origins," review of *The Gosses: An Anglo-Australian Family* by F. Gosse, *Quadrant*, 26:3 (March 1982), 47–50.

"Re-affirming Regularity," review of *Hume and the Problem of Causation* by T. L. Beauchamp and A. Rosenberg, *Times Literary Supplement*, 4116 (February 19, 1982), 182.

"The Sweetest Game," review of *The Penguin Cricketer's Companion* by A. Ross, *Quadrant*, 26:1–2 (January/February 1982), 123.

1983

"English Cottage Gardens," review of *The Cottage Garden* by A. Scott-James, *Quadrant*, 27:5 (May 1983), 76–77.

REPRINTED

D. C. Stove, *Cricket versus Republicanism and Other Essays* (Sydney: Quakers Hill Press, 1995), 106–107.

Bibliography

1985

Review of *Good Thinking* by I. J. Good, *Critical Philosophy*, 2:1 (1985), 85–86.

"Why Have Philosophers?" review of *A History of Philosophy in Australia* by S. A. Grave, *Quadrant*, 29:7 (July 1985), 82–83.

REPRINTED

D. C. Stove, *Cricket versus Republicanism and Other Essays* (Sydney: Quakers Hill Press, 1995), 63–65.

J. Franklin, *Corrupting the Youth* (Sydney: Macleay Press, 2003), 431–433.

Online at www.maths.unsw.edu.au/~jim/whyhave.html

DISCUSSION AND CITATION

D. M. Armstrong, "The 'Form and Pressure' of Australian Philosophy," *Quadrant*, 48:10 (October 2004), 44–45.

1986

"*Et in Arcadia ego*," review of *The Royal Botanic Gardens, Sydney* by L. Gilbert, *Quadrant*, 30:12 (December 1986), 78–79.

1987

"Bombs Away," review of *The Ivory Tower* by A. Kenny, *American Scholar*, 56:1 (Winter 1987), 148–150.

REPRINTED

D. C. Stove, *On Enlightenment* (New Brunswick, N.J., and London: Transaction Publishers, 2002), 155–158.

"An Oxford Companion to *Gardens!*" review of *The Oxford Companion to Gardens* by G. and S. Jellicoe, P. Goode, and M. Lancaster, *Quadrant*, 31:6 (June 1987), 77–78.

1991

Review of *Modern Biology and Natural Theology* by A. Olding, *Australasian Journal of Philosophy*, 69 (1991), 360–362.

D. LETTERS

"Asian Students" [in reply to an earlier *Observer* article and letters
discussing entry standards at Australian universities], *Observer*
(Australia), November 29, 1958, 668.

"Manhattan Moon" [in reply to an earlier *Bulletin* article dated
November 20, 1965, by George McGann, claiming that on the night
of New York's blackout a new moon remained above the horizon
for ten hours], *Bulletin* (Sydney), December 4, 1965, 44.

"The Berkeley Affair" [in reply to an earlier *Vestes* article by a
Professor Bolt discussing events at Berkeley], *Vestes*, 10:1 (March
1967), 38–39; with a reply by Professor Bolt on 39.

DISCUSSION AND CITATION

J. Franklin, *Corrupting the Youth* (Sydney: Macleay Press, 2003),
289.

"Letters to the Editors" [a letter in reply to F. Moorhouse, "The
Importance of the Word 'Berkeley'," *Broadsheet*, 50 (November
1966), 1–6], *Broadsheet* (Sydney Libertarian Society), 51 (May
1967), 9.

"We Shall Miss You" [a letter signed by R. Krygier, O. Harries, and
D. Stove regretting the disappearance of columns by Peter Coleman
and Alan Reid], *Bulletin* (Sydney), February 5, 1972, 7.

"Letters" [a letter in reply to an earlier *Honi Soit* article dated March
6, 1981, interviewing cartoonist Patrick Cook and in which anony-
mous reference is made to Stove], *Honi Soit* (Sydney University),
March 23, 1981, 2.

DISCUSSION AND CITATION

J. Bedford, "Portrait of the Cartoonist," *National Times*,
September 14–20, 1980, 41.

Bibliography

"Karl Popper and Evolutionary Theory" [in reply to an earlier *Kronos* article dated July 1982 discussing Karl Popper's philosophy of science], *Kronos*, 8:2 (February 1983), 81.

"A Man with a Mission" [on Professor Bill Rubinstein's tactics in the campaign to discover war criminals], *Quadrant*, 34:10 (October 1990), 5.

"Smoking Reduces Your Fitness" [on anti-smoking policies], *Quadrant*, 37:12 (December 1993), 6–7.

E. OBITUARIES, REMINISCENCES, AND ADDITIONAL DISCUSSION

D. Waters, "Fathers and Sons – Anderson Betrayed," *Honi Soit* (Sydney University), September 7, 1950, 3; repr. in *Heraclitus*, 59 (July 1997), 3.

A. J. Baker, "Sydney Libertarianism and the Push," *Broadsheet* (Sydney Libertarian Society), 81 (March 1975), 5–10.

H. Feigl, "The Wiener Kreis in America," in *Inquiries and Provocations: Selected Writings, 1929–1974*, ed. R. S. Cohen (Dordrecht: Reidel, 1981), 87.

R. J. Bogdan, *D. M. Armstrong* (Dordrecht: Reidel, 1984), 7, 27, 40.

S. A. Grave, *A History of Philosophy in Australia* (St. Lucia: University of Queensland Press, 1984), 207.

L. Reinhardt, "Science and Truth," *Journal and Proceedings of the Royal Society of New South Wales*, 118 (1985), 129.

R. Brown, "Contemporary Work (1980–1988)," in *Essays on Philosophy in Australia*, ed. J. T. J. Srzednicki and D. Wood (Dordrecht, Boston, London: Kluwer, 1992), 301.

J. A. Burgess, "The Influence of Quine and Davidson on Australian Philosophy," in *Essays on Philosophy in Australia*, ed. J. T. J. Srzednicki and D. Wood (Dordrecht, Boston, London: Kluwer, 1992), 102.

G. Pont, "Don Laycock: Collector and Creator of Dirty Songs," in *The Language Game: Papers in Memory of Donald C. Laycock*, ed. T. Dutton et al., Pacific Linguistics Series C, no. 110 (Canberra: Australian National University, 1992), 643–644.

P. Stavropoulos, "Conservative Radical: The Conservatism of John Anderson," *Australian Journal of Anthropology*, 3 (1993), 78.

Bibliography

D. M. Armstrong, "David Stove, 1927–1994," *Quadrant*, 38:7–8 (July/August 1994), 36–37.

REPRINTED

"David Charles Stove, 1927–1994," *The Australian Academy of the Humanities: Proceedings 1994* (Canberra, 1995), 68–70.

In summary in "David Stove, 1927–1994," *Australasian Journal of Philosophy*, 72 (1994), 410.

In summary in "Professor David Stove," *Sydney University News*, 26:21 (August 17, 1994), 4.

J. Franklin, "Polemicist Divided Friend and Foe," *The Australian*, June 21, 1994, 13.

REPRINTED

"David Stove (1927–1994)," *AAHPSSS Newsletter* (Australasian Association for the History, Philosophy and Social Studies of Science), 48 (August 1994), 11–12; and online at www.asap.unimelb.edu.au/aahpsss/news48/a48_stov.htm

DISCUSSION AND CITATION

B. Oakley, "The End," *The Australian* Magazine, August 5–6, 1995, 46.

B. Kennedy, *A Passion to Oppose* (Melbourne: Melbourne University Press, 1995), 170–171.

J. Ogilvie, *The Push* (Sydney: Primavera Press, 1995), 80–81.

S. Brown, D. Collinson, and R. Wilkinson, *Biographical Dictionary of Twentieth-Century Philosophers* (London: Routledge, 1996), 17, 24.

A. Coombs, *Sex and Anarchy: The Life and Death of the Sydney Push* (Ringwood, Victoria: Viking, 1996), 12–14.

J. McLaren, *Writing in Hope and Fear: Literature as Politics in Postwar Australia* (Cambridge: Cambridge University Press, 1996), 88.

R. J. Stove, "The Prime of Mister Jean Brodie," *Annals Australia*, October 1996, 28–34.

Bibliography

G. B. Harrison, "Living on the Edge," *Heraclitus*, no. 60 (September 1997), 1–2; no. 81 (June 2000), 8–12; and no. 83 (November 2000), 10–13.

C. A. J. Coady, "Australia, Philosophy in," in *Routledge Encyclopedia of Philosophy*, ed. E. Craig (London: Routledge, 1998), vol. 1, 582.

M. Motterlini, *For and Against Method* (Chicago: University of Chicago Press, 1999), 290.

P. P. McGuinness, "We Should Ban Olympics," *Sydney Morning Herald*, April 1, 2000, 46.

A. J. Baker, "Anderson and Andersonians: A History and Analysis," *Heraclitus*, 91 (October 2001), 1–8.

P. Coleman, "Lives of the Young Guns," *Weekend Australian*, August 17, 2002, R10.

G. B. Harrison, *Night Train to Granada* (Sydney: Pluto Press, 2002), 19–23, 132–133.

D. M. Armstrong, "Foreword," in G. Molnar, *Powers: A Study in Metaphysics*, ed. S. Mumford (Oxford: Oxford University Press, 2003), vii.

P. Coleman, "Those Smorgasbord Catholics," *Quadrant*, 47:12 (December 2003), 82–84.

J. Franklin, *Corrupting the Youth* (Sydney: Macleay Press, 2003), 47–48, 60, 105, 108, 113, 131, 141, 158–159, 282–283, 291–294, 299, 306, 308–311.

T. Coady, "From Aquinas to Mabo," review of *Corrupting the Youth* by J. Franklin, *The Age* (Melbourne), February 14, 2004, 5.

P. Coleman, "A Great Editor R.I.P.," *Quadrant*, 48:7 (July/August 2004), 62–63.

D. S. Oderberg, "Hegel Hits the Beach," *Times Literary Supplement*, 5280 (June 11, 2004), 3.

207

Bibliography

Anon. et al., "David Stove," *Wikipedia*, November 28, 2004, and revised significantly since, online at en.wikipedia.org/wiki/David_Stove

B. Attwood, *Telling the Truth about Aboriginal History* (Crows Nest, NSW: Allen & Unwin, 2005), 75.

D. Armstrong, "New Space for Master of Suspicion," *The Australian*, July 13, 2005, 39.

R. Weiss and J. Adams, "Two for the Road," *Sydney Morning Herald*, January 1, 2005, 5.

B. Williams, *Making and Breaking Universities: Memoirs of Academic Life in Australia and Britain, 1936–2004* (Paddington, NSW: Macleay Press, 2005), 102.

J. Franklin, *Catholic Values and Australian Realities* (Bacchus Marsh, Victoria: Connor Court Publishing, 2006), 136.

A. Broadie, *A History of Scottish Philosophy* (Edinburgh: Edinburgh University Press, 2009), 333.

J. Franklin, "The Lure of Philosophy in Sydney," *Quadrant*, 53:10 (October 2009), 76–79.

P. Coleman, "Australian Notes," *Spectator* (Australia), September 25, 2010, V1; and online at www.spectator.co.uk/australia/6298728/part_2/australian-notes.thtml

F. UNPUBLISHED

"The Revolution at Berkeley," 1966.

DISCUSSION AND CITATION

J. Franklin, *Corrupting the Youth* (Sydney: Macleay Press, 2003), 289.

"Equality and Culture," 1990.

"David Armstrong, Challis Professor of Philosophy in the University of Sydney, 1964–91," 1991.

DISCUSSION AND CITATION

J. Franklin, *Corrupting the Youth* (Sydney: Macleay Press, 2003), 299.

"The Hairsbreadth Escape," 1991.

"The Question about Parvus," 1991.

ACKNOWLEDGMENTS

Publication of this book would not have been possible were it not for the care and attention of Anton Garrett of Cambridge and Judith Stove of Sydney. Together they are responsible for ensuring that the manuscript for this essay was not lost following the death of its author in 1994. I am also grateful to James Franklin of the University of New South Wales, who as David Stove's literary executor has put innumerable hours into managing Stove's literary estate, and to Roger Kimball for his vision, skill and prudence as publisher.

I would also like to thank the following people, each of whom has been instrumental in one way or another in the production of this book: David Armstrong, Ermanno Bencivenga, Scott Campbell, Peter Coleman, Sten Christensen, Selman Halabi, Graeme Hunter, Joan Irvine, Jack MacIntosh, Heather Ohle, Emily Pollack, John Russell, Patrick Rysiew, Carl W. Scarbrough, Carol Staswick, Judith Stove, Robert Stove, and David Truelove. Given the many hours of work they have put into the bibliography, James Franklin, Scott Campbell, and Selman Halabi deserve special acknowledgment.

Finally, I would like to record a debt of personal gratitude both to the author of this essay and to the university department where he taught for many years. I first met David Stove when I arrived at Sydney University as a doctoral student in the early 1980s. In the years that followed, I repeatedly had firsthand experience of his generosity. This feature of Stove's character is worth emphasizing in light of how easily the main thesis of the present essay might be misunderstood.

While a student, I also soon realized what a privilege it was for anyone who was serious about studying philosophy to be able to attend Stove's seminars. In fact, my debt of gratitude in this regard quickly came to encompass the entire teaching staff of the university's Department of Traditional and Modern Philosophy, as it was then called. Born in controversy, the department could hardly have been anything but a thorn in the side of university administrators. Even so, as anyone who was lucky enough to have had the privilege of being affiliated with the department before it was disbanded knows, it was an ideal place in which to do philosophy. As Stove himself put it, it was "the best club in the world, and to be or have been a member of it is a pleasure as well as a privilege."*

Trying to articulate exactly why this was so is not an easy task. Partly it was a matter of personalities. Partly it was a matter of people being given the intellectual freedom they needed to find their way. Partly it was simply a matter of people in leadership positions knowing what was important and what was not. But more than anything else, under the leadership of both David Armstrong and David Stove, the department was a place in which *ideas mattered*. To my mind,

---

* David Stove, "David Armstrong, Challis Professor of Philosophy in the University of Sydney, 1964–91," unpublished.

Acknowledgments

for anyone doing philosophy in the shade of Sydney's most famous jacaranda tree during the final decades of the twentieth century, it was this fact and this fact alone that counted the most.

NOTES

INTRODUCTION: COUNTERACTING THE EFFORTS OF THE GOOD

1 Thomas R. Malthus, *An Essay on Population* (1798), ed. M. P. Fogarty, 2 vols. (London: J. M. Dent & Sons; New York: E. P. Dutton & Co. (Everyman's Library), 1958), vol. 2, p. 261.

2 Friedrich A. Hayek, "Why I Am Not a Conservative" (1960), in *The Constitution of Liberty* (South Bend, Ind.: Gateway Editions, 1972), p. 399.

3 Ibid., p. 399.

4 Ibid., p. 398.

5 Ibid., p. 400.

6 Ibid.

7 Ibid., p. 404.

8 Ibid.

9 Ibid.

10 Ibid., p. 400.

11 Ibid.

12 Ibid.

13 Ibid., p. 401.

14 Ibid., p. 400.

15 Ibid., p. 401.

16 Ibid., p. 410.

17 Ibid., p. 401.

18 Ibid., p. 411.

19 David Stove, "Why You Should Be a Conservative," in *On Enlightenment* (New Brunswick, N.J., and London: Transaction Publishers, 2003), p. 172.

20 David Stove, "The Columbus Argument," in *On Enlightenment*, p. 151.

21 John Stuart Mill, *Principles of Political Economy*, bk. 5, ch. 11, §5 (London: Longmans, Green, Reader & Dyer, 1875), p. 571.

22 David Stove, "Living Retired," *Society*, May/June 2003, pp. 78–80.

23 Hayek, "Why I Am Not a Conservative" (note 2), p. 401.

Notes

WHAT'S WRONG WITH BENEVOLENCE

1 Homer, *The Odyssey*, 18, lines 130–37.

2 E. H. Lecky, *A History of European Morals from Augustus to Charlemagne* (1869; London: Watts & Co., 1911), vol. 2, p. 31.

3 David Hume, *An Enquiry Concerning the Principles of Morals* (1751), in *Enquiries Concerning Human Understanding and Concerning the Principles of Morals*, ed. L. A. Selby-Bigge and P. H. Nidditch (Oxford: Clarendon Press, 1975), p. 242.

4 William Godwin, *Enquiry Concerning Political Justice* (1793), ed. I. Kramnick (Harmondsworth, UK, and Baltimore: Penguin, 1976), pp. 772–75.

5 See, for example, references to these writers in G. Lichtheim, *The Origins of Socialism* (New York: Praeger, 1969). John Morley's *Rousseau* (London: Macmillan, 1873) also has useful pages on Morelly (pp. 156–58) and Mably (pp. 184–86).

6 W. E. H. Lecky, *Democracy and Liberty* (London: Longmans, Green & Co., 1896), vol. 2, p. 242.

7 See Lichtheim, *The Origins of Socialism* (note 5). [Also see D. C. Stove, "Did Babeuf Deserve the Guillotine?" in *On Enlightenment* (New Brunswick, N.J., and London: Transaction Publishers, 2003), pp. 3–25. – Ed.]

8 J. J. Rousseau, *A Discourse on the Origin of Inequality* (1755), in *The Social Contract and Discourses*, transl. and ed. G. D. H. Cole (London: J. M. Dent & Sons, and New York: E. P. Dutton & Co. (Everyman's Library), 1913), p. 192.

9 Godwin, *Enquiry Concerning Political Justice* (note 4), pp. 711–12.

10 See Rousseau, *A Discourse on Political Economy* (1758), in *The Social Contract and Discourses* (note 8), p. 254.

11 See, for example, Godwin, *Enquiry Concerning Political Justice* (note 4), pp. 225, 722.

12 See Prosper Enfantin, *The Doctrine of Saint-Simon: An Exposition, First Year, 1828–1829*, transl. G. G. Iggers (Boston: Beacon Press, 1958), the index s.v. "property."

13 Thomas R. Malthus, *An Essay on Population* (1798), ed. M. P. Fogarty, 2 vols. (London: J. M. Dent & Sons, and New York: E. P. Dutton & Co. (Everyman's Library), 1958), vol. 2, p. 54. It is stated in the editor's Introduction (p. vi) that this printing is "based on the seventh edition" (1872). I shall refer to this book henceforth simply as Malthus's *Essay*.

Notes

14 Hume, *An Enquiry Concerning the Principles of Morals* (note 3), p. 194.

15 Most of my information about Townsend's book is drawn from E. Halévy, *The Growth of Philosophic Radicalism*, transl. M. Morris (London: Faber & Faber, 1934), pp. 228–30.

16 Joseph Priestley, *Writings on Philosophy, Science and Politics*, ed. J. A. Passmore (New York: Collier Books, 1965), pp. 183–84. The italics do not appear in the original.

17 Sir G. Nicholls, *A History of the English Poor Law* (London: John Murray, 1854), vol. 2, pp. 175–76.

18 Malthus's *Essay*, vol. 2, p. 48 (italics added). The two arguments referred to in my next sentence are given in the paragraph from which this quotation comes and the following one.

19 Cf. Malthus's *Essay*, vol. 2, p. 51, where Malthus refers to his second argument as pointing out "the *radical* defect" (italics added) of the Poor Laws.

20 Malthus's *Essay*, vol. 2, p. 49.

21 Malthus's *Essay*, vol. 2, p. 46.

22 Malthus's *Essay*, vol. 2, p. 51.

23 Malthus's *Essay*, vol. 2, pp. 55–56.

24 Malthus's *Essay*, vol. 2, p. 236.

25 Malthus's *Essay*, vol. 2, p. 6.

26 Malthus's *Essay*, vol. 2, p. 28.

27 Malthus's *Essay*, vol. 2, pp. 53–54.

28 Malthus's *Essay*, vol. 2, p. 232.

29 Malthus's *Essay*, vol. 2, pp. 223–25.

30 Malthus's *Essay*, vol. 2, pp. 225–32.

31 Thomas Paine, *The Rights of Man* (1791–1792), Part 2, ch. 5.

32 Malthus's *Essay*, vol. 2, p. 190.

33 Malthus's *Essay*, vol. 1, pp. 184–85.

34 Malthus's *Essay*, vol. 2, pp. 216–22.

35 Malthus's *Essay*, vol. 2, pp. 242–44.

36 Malthus's *Essay*, vol. 2, pp. 212–15.

37 Malthus's *Essay*, vol. 2, p. 261.

38 Malthus's *Essay*, vol. 2, p. 212.

39 C. A. Nordhoff, *The Communistic Societies of the United States* (1875; New York: Dover, 1966).

40 J. H. Noyes, *History of American Socialisms* (Philadelphia: Lippincott & Co., 1870).

41 See M. L. Carden, *Oneida: Utopian Community to Modern Corporation* (Baltimore: Johns Hopkins Press, 1969).

Notes

42 A. W. Benn, *History of English Rationalism in the Nineteenth Century* (London: Longmans, Green & Co., 1906).

43 J. M. Robertson, *History of Free-Thought in the Nineteenth Century* (London: Rationalist Press Association, 1929; repr., London: Dawsons of Pall Mall, 1969).

44 By contrast, it was visibly the case that "national socialism" had not been impelled by benevolence, and that it was visibly less socialist than it was national; hence its profound lack of appeal to Enlightened people.

45 For example, see Francis Fukuyama's article "The End of History?" in *National Interest* (Washington, D.C.), 16 (Summer 1989), pp. 3–18. [See also D. C. Stove, "The End of History?" *National Interest*, 17 (Fall 1989), pp. 97–98; as well as Francis Fukuyama, *The End of History and the Last Man* (New York: Free Press, 1992). – Ed.]

46 Malthus's *Essay*, vol. 2, p. 64.

47 Malthus's *Essay*, vol. 2, p. 222.

48 G. J. Holyoake, *Sixty Years of an Agitator's Life* (London: T. Fisher Unwin, 1892), vol. 1, p. 173.

49 See Madeline Gray, *Margaret Sanger* (New York: Richard Marek Publishers, 1979). [Also see D. C. Stove, "O Pioneers! . . . ," *Encounter*, 74:5 (June 1990), pp. 38–40; repr. as "Glimpses of Pioneer Life," in *On Enlightenment* (New Brunswick, N.J., and London: Transaction Publishers, 2003), pp. 111–17. – Ed.]

50 See Holyoake, *Sixty Years of an Agitator's Life* (note 48), vol. 2, pp. 19–25.

51 See Phyllis Grosskurth, *Havelock Ellis* (London: Allen Lane, 1980).

52 See Lecky, *A History of European Morals from Augustus to Charlemagne* (note 2), vol. 2, p. 49, f.n. 3.

53 For example, see A. Solzhenitsyn, *Lenin in Zurich*, transl. H. T. Willetts (London: Bodley Head, 1976), p. 253ff.

54 See Malthus's *Essay*, vol. 2, pp. 216–17.

55 Cf. the extremely arresting passage in Godwin, *Enquiry Concerning Political Justice*, (note 4), pp. 148–49, about the human race having lived, until the Enlightenment, "in a madhouse, and superintended by a set of three or four keepers."

INDEX

Index

INDEX

Index

Index

A NOTE ON THE TYPE

WHAT'S WRONG WITH BENEVOLENCE *has been set in Monotype Fournier, a type modeled on the faces cut in the eighteenth century by Pierre-Simon Fournier. Something of a polymath among typefounders, Fournier made a significant contribution to the typographic arts, designing not only roman and italic text faces, but script types, ornamental and initial letters, types for musical notation, and a wealth of ornaments and vignettes. Fournier's work was expansively displayed in his justly famous* Manuel Typographique *(1764), which combined his types and ornaments in one of the most ambitious displays of typographic finesse of its day. Revived by Stanley Morison during the 1920s, Fournier are notable for their crisp drawing, narrow set width, and perpendicular shading.*

DESIGN & COMPOSITION BY CARL W. SCARBROUGH